Space
Vehicles

Patricia Walsh

Illustrations by Mark Adamic

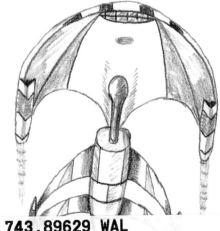

Heinemann Library
Chicago, Illinois

©2001 Reed Educational & Professional Publishing
Published by Heinemann Library,
an imprint of Reed Educational & Professional Publishing,
Chicago, IL
Customer Service 888-454-2279

Visit our website at www.heinemannlibrary.com

Designed by Meighan Depke
Illustrated by Mark Adamic
Photos by Kim Saar, p. 4; Tom Ferry, p. 5
Printed in China

05
10 9 8 7 6 5 4 3

Library of Congress Cataloging-in-Publication Data
Walsh, Patricia, 1951-
    Space vehicles / by Patricia Walsh ; illustrations by Mark Adamic
       p. cm-- (Draw it!)
    Includes bibliographical references and index.
    Summary: Presents instructions for drawing various space craft and vehicles, real and imaginary.
    ISBN 1-57572-350-6   ISBN 1-58810-294-7 (pbk. bdg.)
    1. Space vehicles in art--Juvenile literature. 2. Drawing--Technique--Juvenile
literature. [1. Space vehicles in art. 2. Drawing--Technique.] I. Adamic, Mark, 1962-ill.
II. Title

    NC825.S58 W35 2000
    743'.896294--dc21   00-025405

Some words are shown in bold, **like this.** You can find out what they mean by looking in the glossary.

Contents

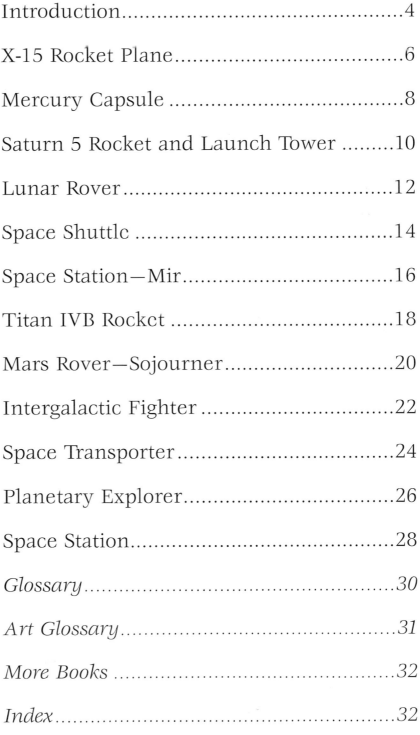

Introduction

Would you like to improve the pictures that you draw?

Well, you can! In this book, the artist has drawn pictures of space vehicles. He has used lines and shapes to draw each picture in small, simple steps. Follow these steps and your picture will come together for you too.

Here is advice from the artist:

- Always draw lightly at first.

- Draw all the shapes and pieces in the right places.

- Pay attention to the spaces between the lines as well as the lines themselves.

- Add details and **shading** to finish your drawing.

- And finally, erase the lines you don't need.

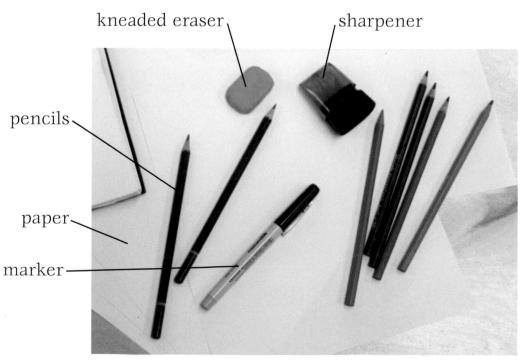

You only need a few supplies to get started.

There are four things you need for drawing:

- a pencil (medium or soft). You might also use a fine marker or pen to finish your drawing.
- a pencil sharpener
- paper
- an eraser. A **kneaded eraser** works best. It can be squeezed into small or odd shapes. This eraser can also make pencil lines lighter without erasing them.

Now, are you ready? Do you have everything? Then turn the page and let's draw!

*The drawings in this book were done by Mark Adamic. Mark started out by **doodling** in elementary school. In college, he studied art and history. Now he works full time as an illustrator, but his hobby is drawing airplanes. Mark's favorite plane is the P-51 Mustang. His advice to anyone who wants to become an artist is, "Don't just draw your favorite thing. Draw everything, because that's the way you learn. Draw every day, and study other artists."*

Draw an X-15 Rocket Plane

In the 1960s, X-15 test pilots flew to the edge of the earth's atmosphere. The X-15s flew at **supersonic** speeds. These test flights provided new information about spacecraft and the upper **atmosphere.**

1 Draw a long oval shape like an ice-cream stick. Make one end pointed for the nose.

2 Add a bump to the top of the pointed end for the pilot's **canopy**. Add one wing and one **tailplane**. Make their shapes short and narrow to show that they are pointed toward you.

3 Draw a short line across the tip of the nose. Draw a small rectangle on the bump for a **cockpit** window. Draw a long oval on the side for the rocket engine. Add a short, straight line to the tailplane.

4 Draw a curved line under the cockpit window. At the round end, draw a rectangular shape above the body and a smaller rectangular shape below for the fins.

5 Draw a small rectangle, a larger triangle shape, and a tiny triangle along the side. Add a tiny triangle behind the canopy. Add **horizontal** lines and a small, backward F-shape to the large rear fin.

6 Write **NASA** between two **parallel** lines on the upper fin. **Shade** the plane and the cockpit window. Darken the areas underneath the body of the plane.

 Draw a Mercury Capsule

The first manned spacecraft of the United States was the tiny Mercury **capsule.** In 1961, **astronaut** Alan Shepard made the first U.S. manned space flight. In 1962, John Glenn became the first American to orbit Earth.

1 Draw a bell shape. Draw a large oval at the end of the bell to make the **heat shield.**

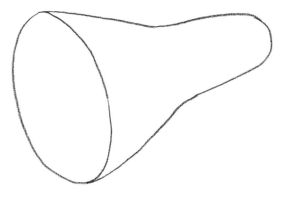

2 Draw a circle near the center of the heat shield. Draw two curved lines across the handle of the bell shape to divide the capsule into three sections.

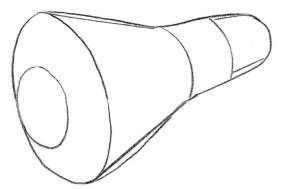

3 Add three small cone shapes and a curved line to the circle on the heat shield. The cones are **retrorockets.** Draw a small circle on the large section for the astronaut's window. Add two curved lines to the handle of the bell shape.

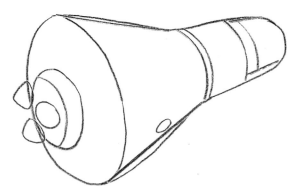

8

4 Add half a square around the tiny window. Draw three small ovals between the retrorocket cones. Make a little C-shape on the top of each retrorocket.

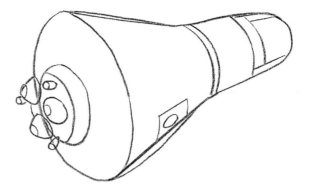

5 Draw two pairs of double lines on the heat shield. Add a straight line to the large section, five **parallel** lines to the middle section, and a line and a circle to the end section.

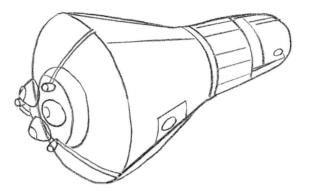

6 Draw several straight lines the length of the large section. Then add lots of short lines in the spaces between the longer lines. Add soft **shading** and darken the important lines.

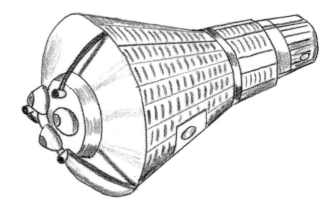

Draw a Saturn 5 Rocket and Launch Tower

It took the powerful Saturn 5 rocket to boost men to the moon in 1968. The first two **stages** carried fuel to launch the rocket. The third stage provided the power to put the Apollo spacecraft into moon **orbit**.

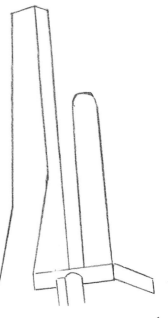

1 Draw a tall box that is wider at its base to make the launch tower. Draw a very short box next to the base for the launch pad. Draw a thin tube with a thicker one next to it just below the base of the launch pad. Draw a tall tube on top of the launch pad for the rocket.

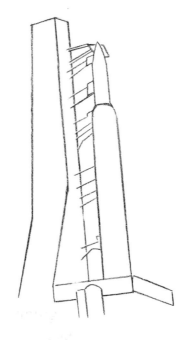

2 Draw a bullet-shape on top of the rocket. This is the third stage of the rocket. Add nine pairs of short straight lines between the launch tower and the rocket.

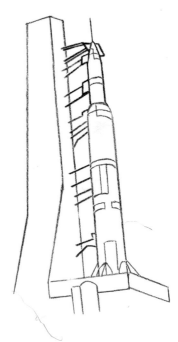

3 Draw three triangular shapes at the base of the rocket. Draw a needle point on top. Add curved lines and rectangles to the side of the rocket.

Add a thin triangle to the top of the launch tower. Draw a line down the side of the tower. Make straight lines across the tower to divide it into many sections. Then add short **vertical** lines to the sides of the launch pad.

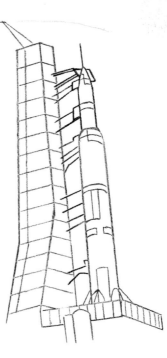

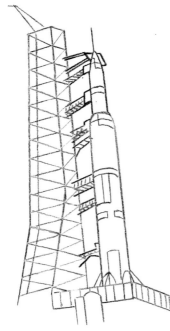

 Draw a **diagonal** line through each section of the launch tower. Use short lines to fill in the spaces between the line pairs that connect the tower and the rocket.

 Darken some of the rectangular markings on the rocket. Add **shading** to the rocket and the launch pad.

Draw a Lunar Rover

The **Lunar** Rover was a lightweight electric car. Apollo **astronauts** first used it on the moon in 1971. The rover helped them explore the surface and collect moon rocks.

1 Start with two circles for the wheels. Connect them with two straight lines to make the rover's frame. Draw curved lines over the wheels to make **fenders.**

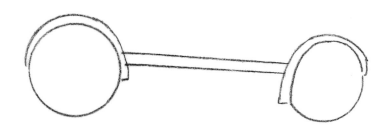

2 Draw three circles, one inside the other, on the wheels. Add a triangle near the middle of the frame. Draw a seat above the triangle. The seat, steering box, and batteries are different-sized rectangles along the frame.

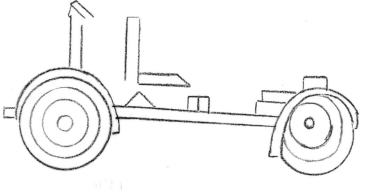

3 Add **cross-hatching** to the seatback. Use tall rectangles to draw racks for equipment, tools, and sample bags behind the seat. Above the front wheels, draw a dish-shaped antenna on a pole.

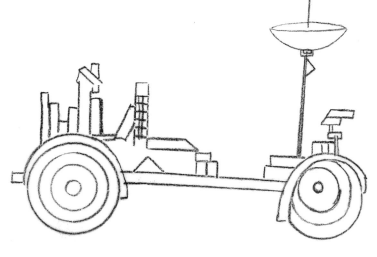

Near the center in front of the seat, use rectangular shapes and straight lines to draw the navigation system and controls. Draw two parts of a circle for the far front wheel.

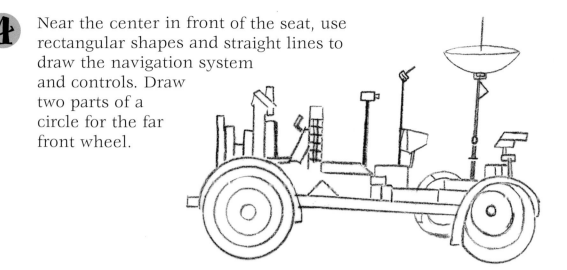

Add straight line details to the wheels and the frame. Draw a half circle next to the seat and two levers on top of it.

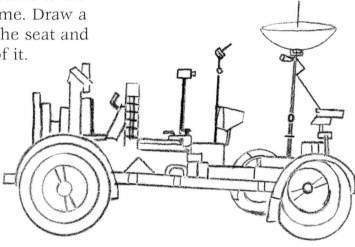

Draw a Z-shape line from the antenna to a camera. Draw short lines around the rims of the wheels. Add **shading** to the seat back and wheels.

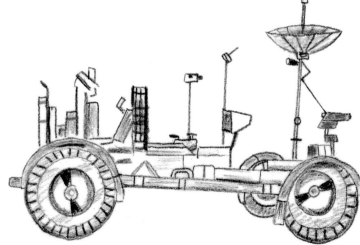

Draw a Space Shuttle

The first Space Transportation System, or space shuttle, was launched in 1981. This reusable spacecraft has made many trips to space. **Astronauts** on board launch, bring back, and repair satellites. They also perform scientific experiments.

1 Draw a rectangle for the body of the shuttle, but make one end rounded and narrower than the rest of the rectangle. Draw a square at the other end.

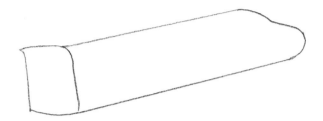

2 Draw a triangular wing along the side. Only one wing can be seen in this picture. Extend the end of the shuttle with a line at the top and two lines at the bottom. These will be **engine bays.**

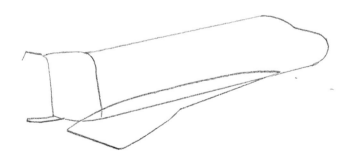

3 Draw three cup-shaped main engines on the end. Draw a smaller cup shape next to them for the control **thruster.** Add a triangle with the tip clipped off above the end. This is the tail.

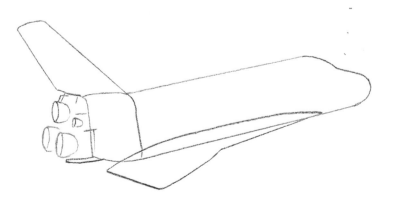

4 Use a straight line to divide the tail for a rudder. Draw a **horizontal** line on the ends. Then draw a line across the end of the wing for a wing flap. Add three small rectangular windows above the nose.

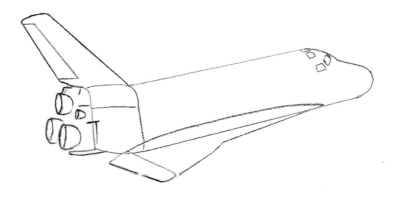

5 Draw a line along the tail, end, and wing edge. Draw a line along the side of the shuttle. End the line behind the windows and make a sharp angle to the top. Use twelve dots to mark door hinges. Draw three short lines like a Z on the nose.

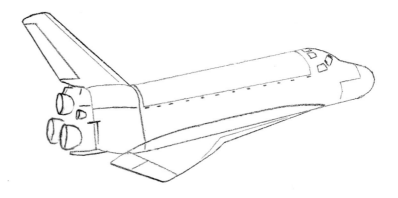

6 **Shade** the nose and the lines on the tail and wings. Shade the windows and the engine bay area. Write **NASA** on the wing and United States on the side. Add the American flag.

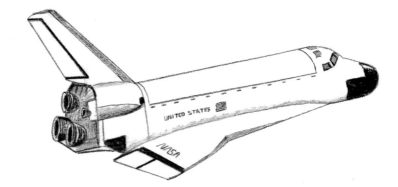

Draw a Space Station—Mir

The former Soviet Union launched the first **module** of the space station Mir in 1986. Over the years, Mir grew as modules were added. **Astronauts** from many countries spent time on Mir collecting data on living in space.

 1 Draw a cylinder with one curved end and one circle end. Draw an oval to the left side. Draw another oval to the right side. These are the space station modules.

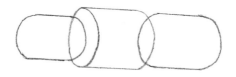 **2** Add a circle to the left. Draw a curved line on the right oval. Then draw a bullet-shaped tube to the right. Draw a curved line across this shape, too.

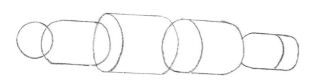

 3 Draw five different rectangles. Three go on the second module and two go on the end module. These are **solar panels.**

Draw two full circles
and one partial circle
on the first module.
These are **docking
ports.** Add small
circles and curved
and straight lines to
the next two modules.

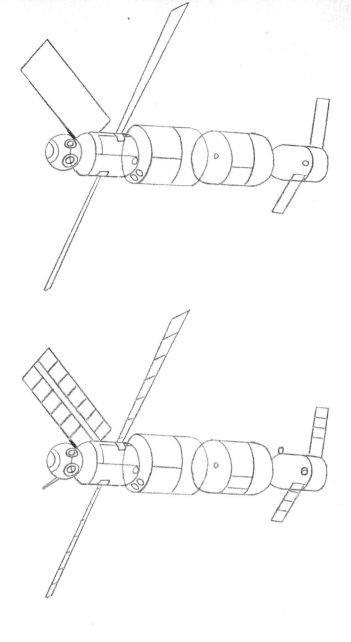

 Divide the biggest
solar panel in half
lengthwise with two
parallel lines. Draw
short straight lines
across the solar
panels. Add a thick
short line to the end
of the first module.

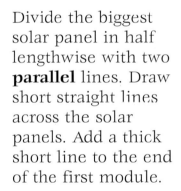

6 **Shade** the docking
ports. Add light
shading to the rest
of the body. Leave
some white areas
to show a gleam.

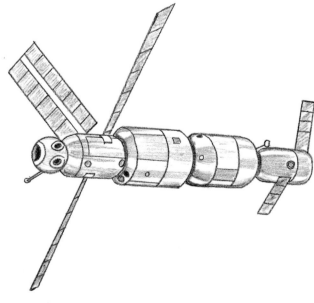

Draw a Titan IVB Rocket

The Titan family of rockets has been around since 1955, but this upgraded and more powerful Titan IVB first flew in 1997. It is an unmanned space booster used by the U.S. Air Force. Its job is to lift heavy satellites into space.

 1 Draw three tubes next to each other. Make the middle tube longer than the two side tubes.

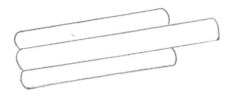

 2 Draw half an oval on the end of each shorter tube. Add a large oval to the end of the middle tube.

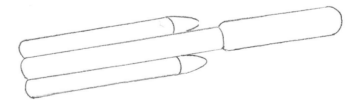

 3 Add half a pointed oval to make the nose cone on the middle tube. Draw half a rectangle on the bottom tube.

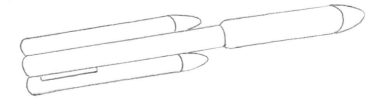

4 Draw C-shapes at the left end of each tube. Add three curved lines, one across the tip of the nose and two near the center of the middle tube. Draw a line down the center of the forward tube to divide it in half.

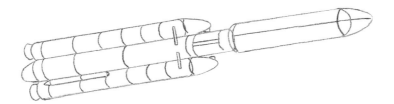

5 Draw seven curved lines across each shorter tube. Draw five curved lines across the middle tube. Connect the tubes to each other with two thick lines near the tops of the shorter tubes. Draw two short **parallel** lines on the middle tube.

6 **Shade** all the rocket ends. Add three streams of rocket exhaust to make the Titan IVB look as if it is roaring through the **atmosphere.**

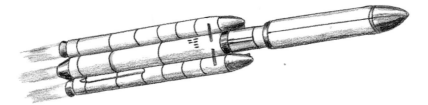

Draw a Mars Rover–Sojourner

When the Mars space **probe** landed in 1997, it set down the Mars rover named Sojourner. This six-wheeled rover collected information about Martian rocks, soil, and dust and sent the information back to scientists on Earth.

1 Draw a row of three circles. Draw a **horizontal** line above the circles. Draw short angled lines at each end of the line.

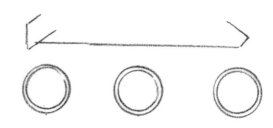

2 Draw half circles above each circle to make thick wheels. Draw small Cs for the wheel hubs. Connect each wheel to the bottom of the rover with short lines.

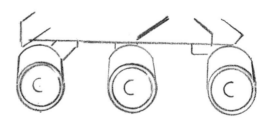

3 Draw a large rectangle above the wheels. Add two short **vertical** lines to the right side to connect it to the bottom of the rover.

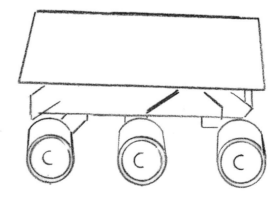

4 Notch out the two corners on the left side of the rectangle by drawing two shapes that are like wide Vs. Draw four **parallel** lines across the rectangle. Then add short lines across each wheel.

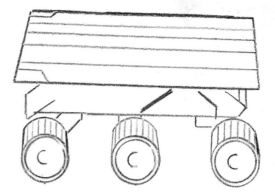

5 Draw parallel lines across the rectangle to make a **crosshatch** pattern for the rover's **solar panel**. Use four short lines to draw the antenna on the upper left-side corner.

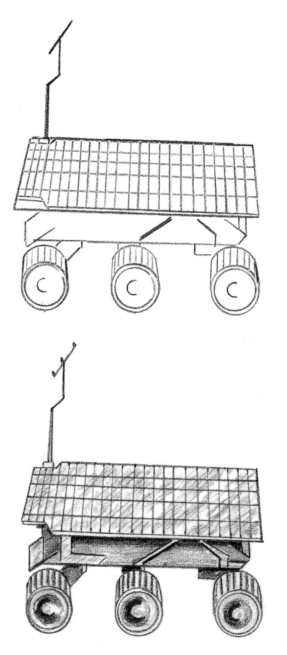

6 **Shade** the wheels and the bottom of the rover. Lightly shade the solar panel. Leave some white to show a gleam.

Draw an Intergalactic Fighter

The artist used his imagination to draw an imaginary high-speed space fighter. He calls it CimAdam MKI, or the "Double Gull." You can copy this design or make your own imaginary fighter.

1 Draw a dart shape with one pointed end to make the body. Draw four diamond shapes, two on top and two below, to make four wings.

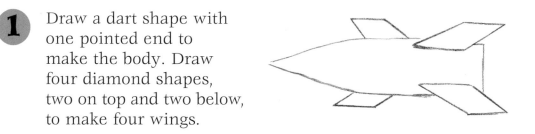

2 Add a thin, needle-like **horizontal** line to the edge of each wing.

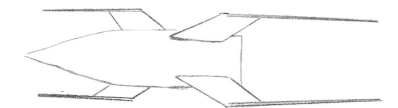

3 Draw a short line on the pointed nose and a half-rectangle shape on the side. Add a narrow rectangle to the top. Draw two **parallel** lines on the side between the two wings.

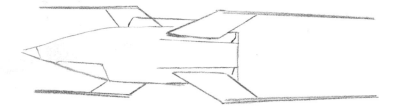

4 Draw diamond shapes at the ends of each needle line. Add a rectangle and a triangle on the nose for windows. Connect the two parallel lines on the body with a curve. Draw a half-rectangle on the bottom of the fighter.

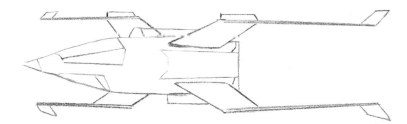

5 Draw a tiny rectangle on the nose and a triangle under the windows. Draw a line on the body just behind the **cockpit** windows. Add ovals to the top wings. Darken the short curved line on the body and make a small triangle at the top just behind the cockpit.

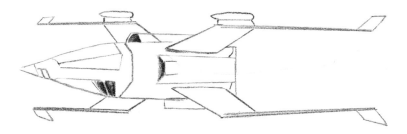

6 Darken the cockpit windows. Leave a thin line of white for the gleam in the glass. Add **shading** under the body of the fighter and your own markings.

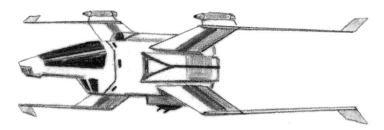

Draw a Space Transporter

The artist calls his imaginary space transporter the FHF-3ST. It will carry heavy cargo over long distances in space. It is the delivery truck of the stars. You can copy the design for this space transporter or design your own.

1 Start by drawing an umbrella shape. Give it a straight handle by drawing a shape a little like an ice-cream stick.

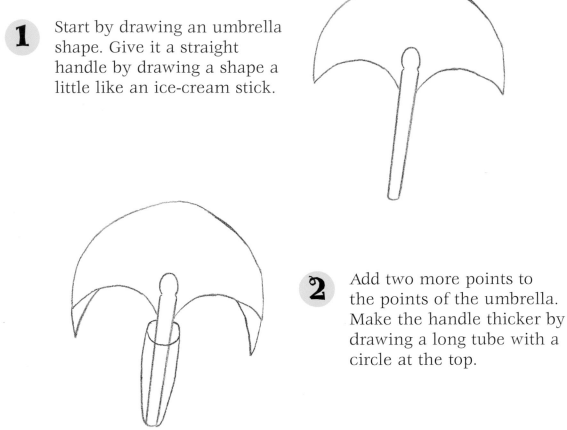

2 Add two more points to the points of the umbrella. Make the handle thicker by drawing a long tube with a circle at the top.

3 Draw a curved line above the top of the umbrella shape and round off the first points you drew. Add two curved wing shapes on either side of the handle. Make them end in sharp points.

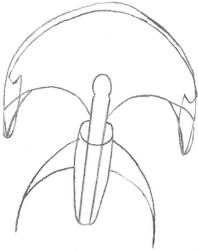

4 Draw a second set of pointed wings on either side of the handle. Add a tiny curve near the end of the handle.

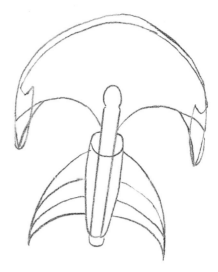

5 Draw thin ovals to connect the tips of the pointed wings. Add three more curved lines across the handle. Add two long curved lines to the umbrella shape. Connect them with one smaller curved line near the top. Make tiny curved lines at the tips of the top wings.

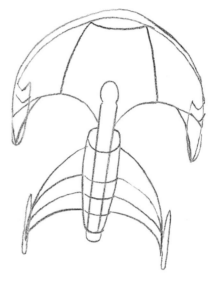

6 Add another curved line just in front of the top curve. Make two rectangles and two squares, and fill them in. Lightly **shade** the left and right sides of the curved wing, just above the side engines, to show depth. Add your own details, markings, and shading. Add rocket exhaust from the engines.

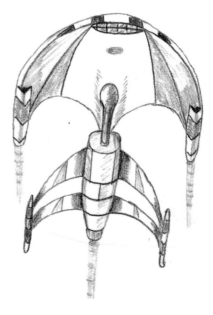

Draw a Planetary Explorer

Already, unmanned space **probes** visit distant planets and moons. But how will people explore space in the future? The artist has imagined this vehicle. He calls it the TGEV for **Terrestrial Geological** Exploration Vehicle.

 1 Draw two larger ovals next to each other. Connect them with half a smaller oval in the middle.

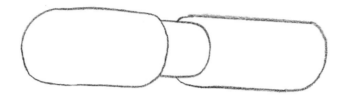

2 Add two curved bumps to the top and two short lines to the bottom. Attach half an oval on the end to the right. Draw a small oval shape underneath.

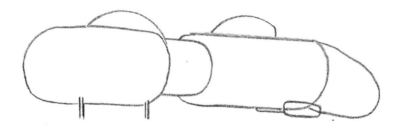

 3 Add two tiny wheels to the ends of the two short lines. Draw a line around these two front wheels to make a belt. Draw three small rectangular shapes in front of these wheels. Then draw two larger wheels under the back end.

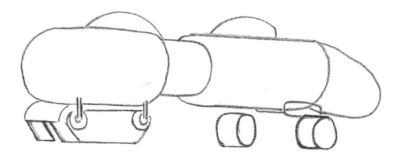

4 Add a big oval windshield and two small side windows. Draw a rectangle around one window for the door. Add little circles inside the belt for the wheels. Draw curved lines on the middle section and short, straight lines under the rear section to connect the wheels.

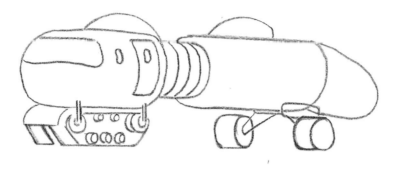

5 Add little oval headlights to the front. Draw a few **vertical** detail lines under the headlights. Draw short lines on the rectangles in the front. Divide the bumps on top with curved lines. Add curved lines and circles to the rear section. Add tread to the wheels and belts.

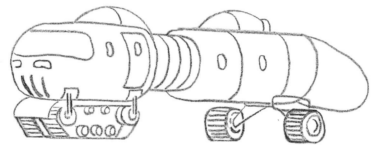

6 Add a pole-like crane to the side of the second bump on top. Darken the windows. Leave a little white in the windows to make it look like space-age glass. Add your own details and **shading.**

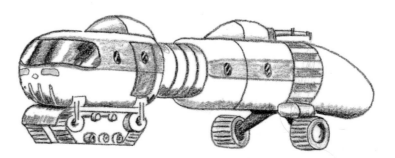

Draw a Space Station

Someday more people may live and work in space. The artist imagines that a future space station could look like this one. Like the real space station Mir, the **modules** of this station would be put together in space.

1 Draw a circle. Draw a narrow tube on either side. Then add a larger oval to the oval on the left. This makes four modules.

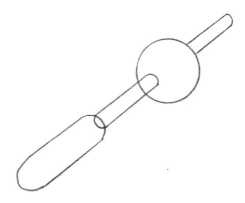

2 Add another oval to the tube on the right. This makes the fifth module. Add a small circle to the top of the round module. Add half an oval to the bottom of the round module and a tiny half-rectangle to each side.

3 Draw a small oval and a long rectangle to each side of the round module to make **solar panels.** Add a small circle to the top of the space station. Use **parallel** lines to add four posts to the sides of the first module.

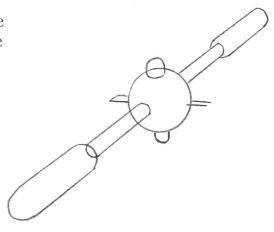

4 Add a small oval to the end of each post to make docking posts for other space vehicles. Add two more rectangular solar panels below the first two you drew. Use two tiny lines to connect the two small circles above the round module.

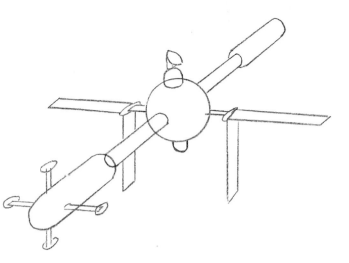

5 Add two curved lines across the round module. Draw a small arrow at the top of the smallest circle on top of the round module. Draw short lines across each end module. Fill in each of the four solar panels with short parallel lines.

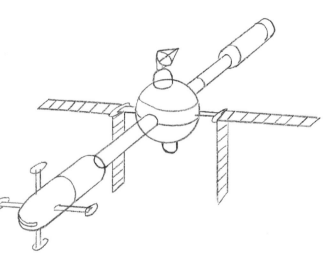

6 Add dots to the end modules to make windows. Add larger dark rectangular bands of windows to the round module. Draw a small curved line that connects the points of the arrow at the top of the space station. Add your own details and **shading.**

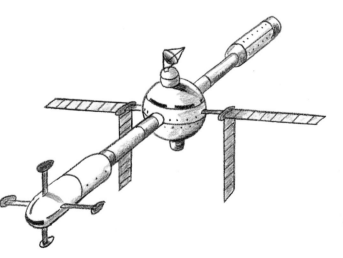

Glossary

astronaut crew member on a U. S. spacecraft

atmosphere gases, such as oxygen and nitrogen, that surround Earth

canopy sliding cover over the part of an airplane where the pilot sits

capsule front section of a rocket that carries crew members and instruments into space

cockpit place where the pilot sits in an aircraft

docking port part of a space station to which visiting spacecraft can connect to unload people and equipment

doodling making little drawings at the edges of paper; cartooning

engine bay compartment on the spacecraft that holds the engine

fender frame over the wheel of a vehicle that protects the wheel and prevents splashing

geological having to do with the rock formations of an area

heat shield barrier that protects a space capsule as it comes in contact with the gases that surround Earth

lunar having to do with the moon

module self-contained unit, or part, of a larger system

NASA National Aeronautics and Space Administration, a United States agency that directs aerospace research

orbit path around a body in space; or to travel around a body in space

probe unmanned spacecraft that carries instruments to collect information

retrorockets small rocket at the front of a rocket or spacecraft that helps reduce speed when landing

solar panel device that collects heat from the sun in order to turn it into energy

stage section of a rocket that has its own engine and fuel

supersonic moving faster than the speed of sound

tailplane tail including the fins and rudder, which is used for steering aircraft

terrestrial having to do with land

test pilot pilot who flies new or experimental aircraft to check their performance

thruster exhaust that adds power to an aircraft's flight

Art Glossary

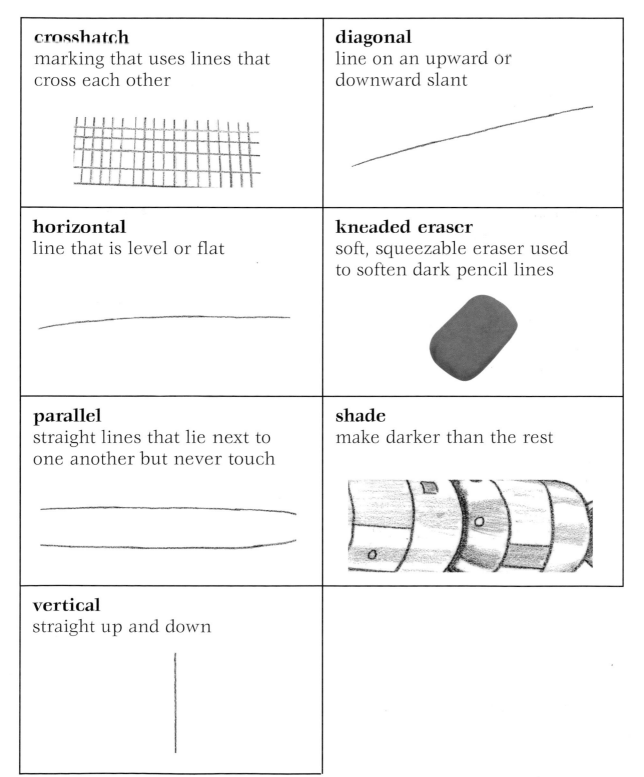

crosshatch
marking that uses lines that cross each other

diagonal
line on an upward or downward slant

horizontal
line that is level or flat

kneaded eraser
soft, squeezable eraser used to soften dark pencil lines

parallel
straight lines that lie next to one another but never touch

shade
make darker than the rest

vertical
straight up and down

More Books

Books about Drawing

Renaigle, Damon J. *Draw Alien Fantasies.* Columbus, N.C.: Peel Productions, 1997.

Tallarico, Tony. *I Can Draw Spaceships, Aliens, & Robots.* Madison, Wis.: Demco Media, Ltd., 1998.

Books about Space Vehicles

Armentrout, Patricia. *Extreme Machines. . .In Space.* Vero Beach, Fla.: Rourke Press, Inc., 1998.

Barrett, Norman S. *Space Machines.* Danbury, Conn.: Franklin Watts, Inc., 1994.

Davis, Amanda. *Space Ships.* New York: Rosen Publishing Group, Inc., 1997.

Richardson, Adele. *Space Shuttle.* Mankato, Minn.: Smart Apple Media, 1999.

Index

TOTAL AIKIDO

T O T A L
AIKIDO

The Master
Course

Gōzō Shioda

with Yasuhisa Shioda

Translated by David Rubens

KODANSHA INTERNATIONAL
Tokyo • New York • London

Originally published in Japanese as *Yoshinkan Aikido Gokui* by Kodansha Ltd., Tokyo.

Photos by Hiroshi Kobayashi and Aikido Yoshinkan.

Distributed in the United States by Kodansha America, Inc., and in the United Kingdom and continental Europe by Kodansha Europe Ltd.

Published by Kodansha International Ltd., 17–14 Otowa 1-chome, Bunkyo-ku, Tokyo 112–8652, and Kodansha America, Inc.

ISBN-13: 978–4–7700–2058–1
ISBN-10: 4–7700–2058–9

First edition, 1996
10 09 08 07 06 05 04   20 19 18 17 16 15 14 13 12 11 10

Library of Congress Cataloging-in-Publication Data
A catalog record for this book is available from the Library of Congress

www.kodansha-intl.com

CONTENTS

KIHON WAZA (BASIC TECHNIQUES) 69

SECTION 4

GOSHIN WAZA
(SELF-DEFENSE TECHNIQUES)   187

SECTION 5

ŌGI (HIDDEN TECHNIQUES)   199

TRANSLATOR'S INTRODUCTION

July 17th 1994, the day that Yoshinkan founder Gozo Shioda Sensei died, was the end of an era. As well as being a recognized master, Gozo Shioda was also one of the last living links between the present generation of aikidoka and the prewar aikijutsu training of Morihei Ueshiba Sensei. It is no exaggeration to state that in watching Shioda Sensei on the mats, we were able to have a glimpse back into history to a time when aikido was still having to prove itself as a fighting art, not yet having gained the recognition and respect that seems so natural to us today. Yoshinkan aikido is perhaps unique in that it can trace its lineage directly back to that prewar period of the *Jigoku Dōjō* (Hell Dōjō), and at the same time be recognized as an aikido style in its own right.

Those of us who were privileged to have been taught by Shioda Sensei will each have our own memories of him, but the common thread among all of those memories, I believe, is the sheer power and energy that he had, and his never-ending enthusiasm for aikido and for life in general.

This book gives the most complete overview of Yoshinkan techniques ever published in English. The secret of training is simple—more training! But in order to really feel the energy of these techniques, it is not enough that the movements are simply copied and repeated. Over and above that, what made Shioda Sensei's aikido so special was the joy and energy he brought onto the mats—the special "X-factor" that cannot be shown in a book like this.

It was Shioda Sensei's great wish in his last years that Yoshinkan aikido would develop and grow to be taught throughout the world. I would like to thank the Yoshinkan Hombu Dōjō for giving me the opportunity to translate this book, and hope that it will help spread the words and techniques of Gozo Shioda Sensei to all who have the hearts and minds to hear their message.

D. R.

PROLOGUE

My father, Gozo Shioda, spent roughly eight years (spanning 1932 to 1941) as a direct student of Morihei Ueshiba, the founder of aikido. As a young man he was initiated into the secrets of "aikido of everyday life." At the first postwar Japanese Martial Arts Exposition, sponsored by the Life Extension Society in 1954, he took the prize for "Outstanding Demonstration" and, encouraged by the support of people from the financial and political world who wanted to see this outstanding aikido spread to a larger audience, founded the Yoshinkan Dōjō.

Yoshinkan, originally named by my grandfather for his dōjō, is also the name that my father gave to his style of martial arts, and means "to cultivate mind and spirit." This name reflects his desire that through aikido, and the mental and spiritual training that goes with it, people will be better able to play a useful role in society.

Yoshinkan Aikido has become well-known throughout the world, and people of many nationalities are training. Every year, the Tokyo Metropolitan Police sends ten of its members (each one at least third dan in kendo or judo) to spend one year as "special students" in the Yoshinkan Headquarters Dōjō in Tokyo. Training in Yoshinkan aikido gives officers the chance to develop and extend their personal and professional skills, and enables them to become aikido instructors in the Women's Police School in Tokyo.

Having mastered the essence of aikido from Ueshiba, my father, Gozo Shioda, demonstrated his aikido in front of the Crown Prince of Japan, Senator Robert Kennedy, and Princess Alexandra among others, and was highly praised by them and by many others who visited his Dōjō.

My father died in 1994, but it is for the purpose of spreading his legacy—these wondrous techniques and spirit—within Japan and throughout the world that this book is being published. If through it even one of its readers will gain a greater understanding of aikido, I will be happy.

Yasuhisa Shioda
August 1995

YASUHISA SHIODA Born 15 November, 1952, Yasuhisa Shioda started practicing aikido at the age of thirteen, training every day. He graduated in 1976 from the Economics Department of Chuo University in Tokyo. As a member of the Yoshinkan Aikido Dōjō he continued to undergo aikido training with his father, and spread aikido by teaching it in universities, and to police departments, and various organizations. From 1984 he spent three years in England, and helped establish the basis for the spread of aikido overseas. After returning to Japan he concentrated on teaching young people, especially nursery school children, originating a unique instruction method that encouraged them to develop their character through the practice of aikido. He also teaches at the community centers. After Gozo Shioda's death in 1994, in order to spread his father's legacy throughout the world, he has been teaching aikido and has also become an author.

How to use this book

In training, Basic Movements and Basic Techniques should be practiced on both the left and the right side, but for the purpose of this book, techniques have been explained and illustrated from one side only.

The person who initiates the attack is called "uke," the person who performs the technique is called "sh'te." In aikido techniques sh'te does not work alone—the next move in each technique is dependent on the situation that uke is in. For that reason there are sections in the text called "Uke's Position," which explain the effect of each of sh'te's movements on uke. These have been added as guides to be used in training.

Movements that frequently reoccur in the Basic Techniques (moving forward, grabbing the wrist, preparatory movements for techniques from the rear, etc.) are explained fully in Section 2. In your basic technique training, please continue to refer to this section.

Although in the text the techniques are broken down into separate movements, it is important to remember that actually these flow into one continuous technique.

For explanation of special terms, please refer to page 28.

In aikido, the use of physical strength (power) has to be very delicate. For that reason, we have deliberately avoided words that might suggest brute force. Please be aware of nuances. (Example: "grasp" as opposed to "grab," or "strike" as opposed to "hit," "punch," etc.)

Techniques are divided into I (ichi) and II (ni). In I techniques, both sides are in the same kamae (right or left) and the flow of energy will be toward uke. In II techniques, partners are in opposite kamae (one in right and one in left), and the flow of energy will be toward sh'te (though there are exceptions to this rule). Usually I is the representative technique, and II is the reverse (turning) technique. There are also a number of techniques that do not have a I or II classification.

THE PRINCIPLES OF AIKIDO

As you get older, your muscles weaken,
And you can no longer lift and pull.
In the end there's a limit to physical strength, no matter how you build it up.
That's why Ueshiba Sensei says that
Unlimited strength comes from breath power.
In effect, it is based on natural principles.
If the other person comes powerfully against you,
And you respond by simply taking his power into yourself,
There is no need for any effort.

— **Gozo Shioda Sayings (I)** —

CHŪSHIN-RYOKU
THE POWER OF THE CENTER LINE

Even when uke resists so that the technique is no longer effective, by locking your hips and maintaining a straight center line, your power will come through.

Keeping your center line straight

One of the basics of aikido is the principle of maintaining a straight center line in the body. For most people, even if they try to stand straight, their center line is not really straight. Even when we do stand straight and focus on keeping our center line fixed, we lose it again as soon as we move. If this happens, then the purpose of aikido, the development of breath power, becomes impossible.

If we are able to maintain a strong center line whatever direction we move in, we have focused power. By forging this focused power, we are also promoting strong posture, concentration, and breath power.

In order to develop focused power the first and essential training is kamae. Once you have attained a stable center in your kamae, you will be able to maintain it in your techniques.

When you have a powerfully focused center line, even if you stand on one leg you will still be able to maintain a centered body.

SHŪCHŪ-RYOKU
FOCUSED POWER

The power that is developed by unifying the whole body

When we use physical strength, we normally assume we are dependent on the power of our muscles. In aikido, however, the power of the hips, legs, knees, abdomen, and so forth, are joined together and are then focused into one point, whether it is the arm or the shoulder or the elbow, and in that way the power we develop is greater than the power of the muscles alone. This power is called shūchū-ryoku, or focused power.

If the body as a whole moves in an unfocused way, this sort of power cannot be developed. By using shūchū-ryoku, all of the power that is brought together from the whole body can be sent out through one point. If one part is too quick, or is late, it will not work. If the whole body is integrated as it moves, its power will be the power of the focused center line concentrated into one point. To put it another way, shūchū-ryoku is chūshin-ryoku at its extreme.

In order to develop shūchū-ryoku, it is important not to depend on the strength of the upper body. If you do use that strength, the flow of energy will be stopped and you will not be able to transmit shūchū-ryoku. Therefore, in developing concentrated power, it is important to ensure that your body is in a relaxed mode.

In aikido techniques, it is entirely through this concentrated power that the power of the techniques is developed. The purpose of training in basic techniques is to establish in the body the ability to produce shūchū-ryoku.

The "trick" to concentrated power is in the big toe. When we fix the big toe to the floor, power comes into the hips. To that power you can then add the acceleration of the "spring" action of the knee. If these movements are all done together, a very powerful force is developed. Because of this, developing the big toes through, for example, kneeling techniques are very important.

①

②

③

One example of shūchū-ryoku. Even using just the index finger, by concentrating your energy you can produce a large amount of power.

KOKYŪ-RYOKU BREATH POWER

Bringing together sensitivity, breathing, and rhythm into a focused power

Breath power is what is developed at the point where our own focused power comes into contact with the other person. Here, the matter of spirit and rhythm (timing) are of basic importance.

The matter of the spirit is how to become "empty." You should lose the feeling of "I will try to do this...I will try to do that..." and instead simply be in a serene state of mind. You will then be able to read the other person's movement and understand the flow of energy. You will then naturally feel where your own line of attack will be.

In this way you can utilize different tempos and rhythms, not moving at one speed, but rather choosing the one that is most applicable to the situation between yourself and uke. Rhythm is a result of your own breathing. By breathing out when you should breathe out, and breath-

ing in when you should breathe in, rhythm is created.

When feeling (sensitivity), breathing, and rhythm are brought together and become one, kokyū-ryoku, or breath power, is born. You and the other person become as one: where you lead you will be able to make uke follow.

It is not necessary to do any special training in order to get breath power, because breath power is something that comes out of your own feelings. If you continue to train conscientiously in the basics, you will eventually realize, "This is breath power." Once you have had that experience, by continuing your training you will increase its occurrence, until eventually it will become constant. Once that has happened, you will experience what Morihei Ueshiba called "becoming one with the universe."

KI

"Ki" is the mastery of balance

In aikido we often use the word "ki," or energy, but this word covers a variety of meanings. "Ki" as it is manifested in the performance of techniques is what we have when the components of correct posture, center line, breathing, the explosive power of focused energy, timing, etc., come together so that we reach the highest state of perfect balance. It might be said that "ki" is "the mastery of balance."

The meaning of "ki" in the phrase "harmonize your ki," refers to sensitivity to your partner, and covers all of the elements that come out of your partner's state of being, so that power, speed, timing, and rhythm are all part of the meaning of ki in this instance.

As you continue your training, you will become more sensitive to how your opponent is going to attack you, which direction he is going to move in, and where he will focus his power. It is possible to say that this ability to "see/feel energy" is one of the major purposes of training.

Delving deeper we see that "ki" is both the matter of the universe, and what controls it. To harmonize with the universe means to be in balance. "Aiki," i.e., "harmonizing of energy," means to lose your own ego; it is the technique of submitting to the natural flow of the universe. By doing that you can effortlessly realize your own natural self depending on the situation that is in front of you, and it is by developing this harmony that we find the realization of aikido.

IRIMI
ENTERING

A body movement that allows you to move in to the side of uke's body

In irimi, or entering, instead of clashing with uke's power straight-on, you move off that line and move in to the side of his body to the "safe angle." By using irimi, you can move your body to a safe position and at the same utilize your partner's power in order to apply a technique.

In irimi it is important that you take a half step forward yourself as your opponent is coming in to attack. Never wait for the attack to come. Because you yourself are moving forward, uke's power is also increased, and by opening up your body at that point the success of the entering movement is brought about. In addition, make sure that, although you are moving straight forward, you are actually moving to the outside of the other person's attack.

As you move forward come to the outside of the other person's punch, and strike up through the jaw in irimi-tsuki.

KAITEN
TURNING

Envelop uke's movement in your own circular movement

In aikido there are not really any straight movements; the basis is circular movements, which allow us to redirect the other person's power without clashing with it. Also, having the ability to make circular movements is more likely to lead to success in getting our own body in close to uke so that we can quickly apply the technique. By enveloping our opponent's movements within our own circular movements we are able to completely take away his power.

Within the circular movements, there are situations in which we are in the center and uke is turned around us, and situations in which uke is at the center, and we move round the line that is the circumference of uke's circle. This circular movement is not always a simple flat circle; there are times when it is a spiral, or when it looks as though it's going around the surface of a ball. Whichever one it might be, a circular movement is one that enables us to redirect the direction of power without interrupting the flow of energy.

In order to perform the *kaiten* movement, it is important for your own center of balance to be firmly fixed. If your own center of balance is wobbly, you will not be able to make a stable turn. Maintaining this strong center of balance is also one of the principles that allows you to smoothly transfer your weight from one foot to the other.

①

Having entered, you can then add the effect of the turn to bring uke sufficiently off-balance, and so can then apply shōmen irimi-nage.

② ③ ④

⑤ ⑥ ⑦

EXTENDING YOUR PARTNER'S BODY

In avoiding the punch, if you completely extend uke's body, even a light touch to his elbow will have a powerful effect.

By causing uke to overextend his energy, you make him powerless

If you can sufficiently blend with uke's energy so that you can "lead" him, at the moment that he becomes overextended and powerless you apply the technique. This is one of the basic principles of aikido.

For example, if you were to stumble and lose your balance, you might soon regain your feet, but if you were to completely trip, then all you could do would be to fall over. Extending uke's body means that you are able to lead uke's body until he is no longer able to maintain control over his own balance. By extending the body and then applying an effective technique, it is possible to cause a potentially highly damaging fall.

In order to achieve that without interrupting uke's energy, you need to lead him so that his energy is always extended beyond his body. Just like pulling on the hand of someone who has already started to fall over, it is important, once you have taken uke's balance away, not to give him a chance to regain his feet.

TIMING

When uke comes to push at your shoulders, at the exact moment that his elbows are extended you use your shoulders to push back. As though he has been thrust with a staff, all of his attacking power is reversed.

Grasp the moment to take over uke's power

The ideal of aikido is to use a small amount of power for a large effect. An important part of achieving this is your timing at the moment that you make contact with uke. However many moves and techniques you remember, if your timing is not correct the technique will be "dead." On the other hand, if you can skillfully blend your timing with uke's attack, even if you do not perform any particular technique, you will still be able to inflict severe damage.

Whether it is blending with your partner when he comes to grab you or strike you or, alternatively, striking him, whatever you do, timing is what gives it life. If your timing is late, you will be crowded out by uke; if you are too early, uke will see your movement and change his attack. You should apply your technique exactly at the moment that he commits himself to the attack—this is proper timing.

Utilizing that split second is what is called "harmonizing." It would be correct to say that in aikido all techniques begin from this idea of 'harmonizing'.

USING YOUR PARTNER'S ENERGY

Catch the timing of the oncoming energy

By using uke's oncoming energy as he comes to grab your hand, you are able to create a situation in which he will become completely powerless. For example, if as uke comes to grab your hand and push it, you blend with that energy and pull your own wrist toward yourself, you will be able to unbalance uke before he is able to withdraw his hand. Alternatively, if he pulls you, if you blend with that and move at the same time, you can utilize his pulling energy.

In the above example, if your timing is late you will lose to uke's energy, and if you are too early uke will release his hand. At the very moment that the power of the grabbing hand is applied, that is when you must use uke's energy. It is no good if you simply pull your hand in. If you are properly focused, you will be able to create a real connection with uke's energy.

If you can control this timing well, at the moment that he is unbalanced uke will unconsciously grab the hand more strongly in order to support his body, and at that moment will not be able to release his grip. Once his grip is strong, you can lead his energy and so come into a technique. Which technique you use depends on the position of the hold. Even if the energy (grip) is fixed, by offering an opening you can blend with uke's power, and you will be able to make use of his energy, as in a pull or push, in the same way.

By using uke's oncoming energy as he comes to grab your hand, you can break uke's balance.

CONTROLLING UKE'S KNEE

When uke grabs our dōgi, by redirecting his power along his weak line, we can unbalance him by way of his knees.

Apply your energy against the weak point

In aikido we have many techniques in which we lock uke's wrist. However, simply locking out the wrist is not enough: we must also apply the technique to uke's lower body, so that uke's knee is knocked away. Thus we are able to see that the technique has had a real effect. For example, in nikajō, if we just lock the wrist and uke has sufficient strength, the technique will not be effective. If, however, we send our energy through the wrist in order to destabilize the knee, even if uke resists we will be able to unbalance him. It is perhaps possible to say that an aikido technique is where we are able to unbalance the other person even without hurting him.

In most cases, when we try to apply a technique, we concentrate only on the place where we think the control will have its effect, and often we try to apply our strength against the angle where uke's power to resist is strongest, so that there is a clash of power. But however strong uke is, there is always one line that is weak. By redirecting the power into that line and thus turning all of uke's power back on himself, he will not be able to keep his feet (stay on balance).

In order to find that line, we must work to improve our overall sensitivity to, for example, how uke looks, his posture, balance, and so forth. In order to achieve that, it is necessary to experience many different sorts of power on our own body.

ATEMI
STRIKING

The moment of contact becomes the strike

The founder, Ueshiba Sensei, said, "In a real battle, atemi is seventy percent, technique is thirty percent." The training that we do in the dōjō is designed to teach us various sorts of techniques, the correct way to move our body, effective ways of using our power, and how to create a relationship with the other person.

In a real battle, we must use the power that we have developed in our bodies in the dōjō and use it explosively in an instant; we must decide the outcome of the fight at that moment. In that situation atemi becomes very important.

In aikido, we don't use any special strength to apply atemi. Just like in all the other techniques, we can generate power through the use of focused energy. For example, in the case of shōmen-tsuki, if you can use the front knee to effectively transfer all of the power of the forward movement of your body, all of the body's energy will be transferred into your fist. Basically, this is the same as the principle of hiriki no yōsei (elbow power movement) (see pages 32–35).

In atemi, timing is of course very important. When uke comes toward you, if you can time it so that you make your strike at the moment that he is off-balance, even without using strength you will be able to hit with great power.

In the case of someone coming to attack you from the rear, if you have an understanding of distance and timing, you can use your back to strike them. This is a variation of atemi.

Strikes as they are used in aikido are not limited to just hitting with the fist or tegatana (side of the hand). If you make contact with uke with focused power, that is atemi, so it is possible to use your shoulder, your back, or any part of your body to make the atemi.

ICHITAITA
ONE AGAINST MANY

Hold an opponent to catch an opponent

One of the distinctive features of aikido is that it is not just used in one-on-one situations but can also be used when facing many opponents. If you are facing multiple attackers it is of course important to maintain your own strong posture, but it is also important to be able to perceive the situation of your opponents.

Each opponent who is facing you is also concentrating on the person opposite him, so his attention is divided. That weakness is where you attack. If you move forward and offer yourself for attack, your opponents will be affected by that and will simultaneously come forward to attack as well, but a tiny time-lag will appear between each of those attacks. If you jump forward at whoever is fastest, and turn your body correctly, that first person will bump into the person opposite him, and they will become confused. Basically, that is the principle of "hold an opponent to catch an opponent." In this way you can create confusion even if there are a group of people facing you.

In the above scene, as you change direction without stopping your movement, your circular body movements will have a great effect. Because of the necessity to react quickly, atemi can be used in many ways as you make your attack.

By moving forward yourself, all of your opponents will also come toward you. At that point, by turning your body you are able to confuse them.

TRAINING SYSTEM

Training begins with basics, and it returns to basics

Kihon Dōsa / Basic Movements

We train in kihon dōsa in order to learn the basic body movements of aikido. There are six basic movements, each one of which can be performed alone or with a partner. They are: hiriki no yōsei ichi (elbow power I), hiriki no yōsei ni (elbow power II), tai no henkō ichi (body change movement I), tai no henkō ni (body change movement II), shūmatsu dōsa ichi (after-class exercise I), shūmatsu dōsa ni (after-class exercise II). Beginners, who usually perform the movements without a partner, learn through them how to focus the power developed by their whole body, how to do entering and turning movements, and how to maintain a stable posture. Higher grades, who perform the movements with a partner, taking on both the role of sh'te and of uke, develop a sense of connecting with the partner's energy. They also learn how to use the partner's weak line in order to unbalance him, how to develop breath power, and so forth.

These movements can be practiced empty-handed or with a sword.

Kihon Waza
Basic Techniques

In Basic Techniques we allow uke to make various attacks (i.e., using his power in different ways), and then use our technique in order to complete the interaction.

● **Suwari waza** (kneeling techniques)—techniques performed when both people are facing each other in a kneeling position. There are as many kneeling techniques as there are standing techniques.

● **Hanmi-handachi waza** (one kneeling, one standing techniques)—techniques performed when sh'te is in a kneeling position, and uke makes his attack from a standing position.

● **Tachi waza** (standing techniques)—techniques performed when both partners are standing.

● **Ushiro waza** ("ushiro" means "behind, rear")—techniques in which uke attacks from the rear.

Suwari waza and hanmi-handachi waza are left over from the palace techniques of the olden times [when the nobility would spend much of their time indoors in a kneeling position], and should be done using shikkō (knee-walking). These techniques contribute greatly to the strength and flexibility of the ankles and hips. They are also very important for getting the body used to the idea of moving from the hips. Once you are able to perform suwari waza, tachi waza will become simple.

Points to remember when performing basic techniques

The movements of the basic techniques are designed specifically to show us how, by using rational methods of guiding energy, we can find a technique that will unbalance our partner. Therefore each movement must be performed correctly, and you should make sure that you do not "make it up" by yourself.

To avoid confusion when performing basic techniques, when you are uke you should not use your power to try to overcome sh'te. Harmonize your breathing with that of sh'te, and allow the technique to be performed correctly. In this way, you too will come to understand the correct way of using your power when performing the technique.

Applied Techniques

These are techniques that have developed out of the basic techniques. While in basic techniques we separate each movement and do it individually, in applied techniques we train by performing the technique in one flowing movement. We are also able to practice applied techniques with weapons such as the bokken (sword) or tantō (knife).

Free-style Techniques

This is training in which the attack your partner is going to make is predecided, for example, shōmen-uchi (front strike) or katate-mochi (one-handed grasp). Your partner continues to attack you in that way while you have the freedom each time to choose which technique to apply. You can use the body movements and the redirection of power that your body has learned through training in the basic techniques while making the realistically continuous movements of the various free-style techniques. You can also expand your training by having your partner use two or three different attacks.

Free-style techniques against multiple attackers

This is where you perform free-style techniques against two, three, or more opponents. It is important to move with the whole of your body, and to move in such a way that you always maintain a stable posture. You can also introduce different attacks by having one opponent attack empty-handed, one attack with a sword, and one with a knife.

Other training

The highest and most difficult level of training is to unbalance someone who has locked out their strength specifically in order to stop you from unbalancing them. In the Yoshinkan, Soke (Headmaster) Gozo Shioda shows how it is done by demonstrating on his senior students.

EXPLANATION OF SPECIAL TERMINOLOGY

Circular

This term is used, for example, in "Raise the tegatana (cutting edge of the hand) in a circular movement," or "Move your leg forward in a circular movement." It means that your movement should describe an arc, not a straight line.

Lock out

For example, "Lock out the wrist," "The elbow is locked out." In this sense, "to lock out" means "to apply pressure into the joint." The meaning, for example, of "Lock out the elbow" is "Apply pressure through the wrist up into the elbow." The purpose of this control is to prevent the particular joint from being able to move.

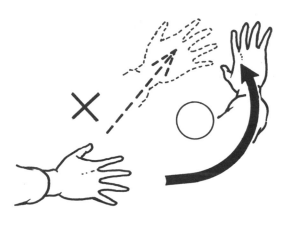

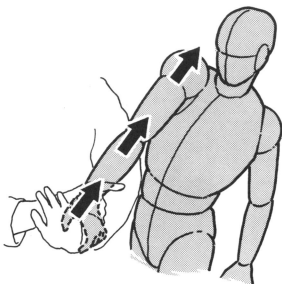

To turn over

For example, "Turn the elbow over," "Turn the shoulder over." It means that you should turn that part over so that it is facing in the opposite direction. Actually, when we say "Turn uke's elbow and shoulder over to the front," what we mean is "Turn uke's arm so that the elbow and shoulder are facing forward, and uke is unbalanced in that direction."

To fix

"Fix your power," "The energy is fixed." Lead uke's power so that it reaches its full extent of movement, at which stage uke loses his ability to pull back or withdraw. By fixing the energy, uke is not able to let go of the hand he has grasped.

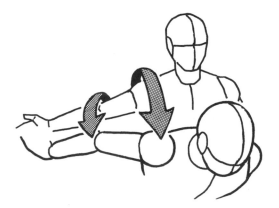

Open up

This usually means either to the right or to the left. "Open up your front foot to the left," means that you move the foot to the left and also turn your body to face that way. "Open up your body to the rear" means that you make a turning movement to the rear with your back foot and also change the direction that your body is facing.

TAI SABAKI NO KIHON
THE BASICS OF BODY MOVEMENT

The basics are only a guiding principle.
Your strongest posture is the one that fits your constitution.
That cannot be taught to you,
You have to find it for yourself.
It is not a question of widening your stance or narrowing it,
If the truth be told.
But, people will do what is comfortable for them,
So if you allow them to, they will just make it up for themselves.
That is why, you must always return to the basics,
This is what is important.

— **Gozo Shioda Sayings (II)** —

KAMAE
BASIC STANCE

The basic posture that will allow you to develop breath power

Originally, there was no position in aikido that might have been called a "basic stance." The founder, Morihei Ueshiba Sensei, while saying that the basic stance was "to open your feet to the six directions [north, south, east, west, up, down]," also wrote, "The complete kamae is what arises from where the gods lead you, depending on time, situation, the lie of the land, the spirit of the moment—kamae is what is in your heart." [from *Budō*], so that the explanation for the real battle is to adapt to the circumstances that you are in.

In the Yoshinkan, in order to learn the stance that is necessary to develop breath power, we introduce kamae as the most basic part of our training.

Through training in kamae, we learn to ❶ maintain a straight balance, ❷ keep our hands, feet, and hips on the center line of the body, ❸ maintain correct posture without having to make an effort, and ❹ extend our spirit forward. For beginners, the stance may feel very unnatural; we train so that eventually the body will come naturally into this position. If you can naturally assume kamae, your body will have started to gain the ability to develop breath power.

When your right hand and leg are forward, you are in right-handed kamae (migi hanmi kamae), and in the opposite position you are in left-handed kamae.

Feet The distance between your feet should be one-and-a-half times the length of your own foot. Both feet should be standing on the same line, with the toes pointed outward, so that if the heel of the front foot and the toes of the back foot came together they would make a right angle. By turning the toes of the front foot outward (and having the balance over the front foot), you are able to make a turning movement more easily. Make sure that neither heel floats up, and press the big toe of each foot firmly into the mat. This is also good training for the big toes, which are so important in maintaining balance.

Knees Lightly bend the front knee, and keep the back knee completely extended so that the back foot snaps into the extended position. Your balance should be sixty percent over the front foot and forty percent over the back foot. You should not be supported by the front knee, but rather the body should extend straight up from the back

foot. The front knee should be loose enough that it can move freely.

Hips Your hips should be stable and facing forward, exactly along the front line of the body. Be careful, as it is easy to open up slightly with the hip on the back leg side.

Upper Body Extend your neck and spine. By extending right through from your back foot to your neck you can ensure that your whole body will be leaning forward in one line. Relax your shoulders, and make sure that you don't open up your armpits. Keeping the neck straight is one of the characteristics of aikido.

Facing your partner in kamae

When facing a partner, *ma-ai* (the correct basic distance) is one tatami, or about 1.8 meters. Although this *ma-ai* might seem large for an empty-handed style, it has a purpose: by leading our opponent into this space we can maintain the initiative.

When facing an opponent, our eye-line is important (i.e., the way we observe our opponent). By focusing on the other person's eyes but maintaining awareness of the whole of his body, we can read his body's movements. As we improve through training, by seeing the changes in his eyes, we will be able to read his next movement and also his state of mind.

Ai-hanmi kamae / mutual kamae

Partners are facing each other in the same kamae. If both sh'te and uke are in right-handed kamae they are in migi ai-hanmi kamae (mutual right-handed kamae), and if both are in left-handed kamae they are in hidari ai-hanmi kamae (mutual left-handed kamae).

Gyaku-hanmi kamae / Opposite kamae

Partners are facing each other in oppositie kamae. When sh'te is in right-handed kamae and uke is in left-handed kamae they are in migi gyaku-hanmi kamae (right-handed opposite kamae), and when sh'te is in left-handed kamae and uke is in right-handed kamae they are in hidari gyaku-hanmi kamae (left-handed opposite kamae).

Hands / Arms Open up the fingers of the hands. Both the upper and the lower hand should be held along the center line. The upper hand should be in line with the chest, and the lower hand should be one fist's length away from the abdomen. Hold both elbows so that they are not overextended. The fingers of both hands should be pointing at the base of your partner's throat. Beginners tend to need strength in order to keep the fingers open, but keep practicing until it becomes natural.

Spirit Your spirit should be sent strongly forward, but you should also have a "still mind" so that you can react appropriately however your opponent might attack you. It is also important that you don't focus only on the person standing in front of you, but maintain all-around awareness.

HIRIKI NO YŌSEI ICHI
ELBOW POWER I

Raise the hands as you are moving forward

Hiriki is an old Japanese expression meaning "elbow power," and in aikido terms it has come to mean "breath power as expressed through the elbows." This elbow power movement is the basic form that we use to teach the body to develop breath power. In the (I) movement, as we move forward and backward, we also learn the movement of raising and cutting down with the hands. The explanation that follows refers to the movement as it is done with a partner.

① Uke approaches from the front diagonal and grasps your lower arm in both of his hands, fixing it so that it is unable to move. If you are in a migi-hanmi kamae, uke grasps firmly with his right hand, and the left hand comes from underneath to assist in the gripping.

②–③ As though extending forward with the hips, slide forward with the front foot. At the same time, with a feeling as though extending forward with the elbows, raise both hands up in a circular movement along the body's center line.

Uke's Position

As sh'te raises his hands, your elbows are raised up.

④ Bring your balance forward strongly over the front knee, and pull your back leg up in its extended position, so that you will be in a leaning-forward position. Once you have raised both hands, the thumb of the upper hand should be in front of the head, and the thumb of the lower hand should be pointing at the nose.

⑤–⑧ Move backward by sliding the back foot to the rear, and cut down with both hands in a circular movement. Pull back the front foot so that you return to your original kamae position. Make sure that your balance doesn't fall back in this position. Repeat the movement.

IMPORTANT POINTS

● Make sure that you don't open up with your hips as you come forward.

● Don't leave your back foot behind you. If your hips are truly facing forward, by pushing forward with your front knee you will naturally be able to pull your back leg up.

● Make sure that you don't have your balance over your back foot as you move forward with your front foot, and also be careful that you don't do the opposite and lean forward so much so that your hips begin to "float."

● Don't lift up the heel of the back foot.

● Don't pay attention to the fact that your arm is being held, i.e., you should do the technique exactly as if you were doing it by yourself.

● Don't lose the distance between your elbows and your body.

● Don't open your elbows to the side, and don't raise your shoulders.

● Don't move in such a way that the different parts of the body move separately. The whole of the body should move in time with your breathing.

Your hands, feet, and hips move in one line

This is how the movement looks when you are doing it alone, as seen from the front. Your hands, feet, and hips all move keeping to the center line of the body, and the body keeps facing straight to the front. In this manner the power from the whole of the body becomes focused, and that power can then be transferred through the hands.

The balance is brought forward by the forward movement of the hips

①–② This movement involves more than just the feet moving forward. As the hips move forward, the balance is also brought forward. At the same time, the back foot is planted into the mat as though thrusting back with a jō (wooden staff). In order to do this, the back foot has to be absolutely extended, so that the back knee is completely locked out and the back of the foot is fixed to the mat—this is the basis of the movement.

③ Once the balance is sufficiently over the front foot, push the front knee forward. Even when the movement of the front foot has stopped, the hips should continue to move forward, so that the balance is also being pushed forward. In order to achieve this, it is important that the front knee moves forward in a full movement. By pushing the front knee forward in this way, the back foot will naturally be pulled up.

HIRIKI NO YŌSEI NI
ELBOW POWER II

As you transfer your weight, raise the hands

①   ②   ③

⑦   ⑧   ⑨

This is the movement that you apply when the hand that is down by the side of your body is grasped; to raise the hands, you use the power that is generated by transferring your weight and changing the direction of your body. In aikido we don't just use the power of the arms, but rather we use the power generated by transferring the weight in executing the technique. Beginners easily lose balance as they are making this transferring movement. Hiriki no yōsei ni is therefore designed to teach us how to transfer the weight while maintaining a stable posture and without losing balance. It is also very effective at increasing the flexibility and strength of the feet and hips. The explanation that follows refers to the movement as it is done with a partner.

①–② From the same position as in (I), when the hand has been gripped, turn around, keeping the balance over the toes of both feet, so that the body turns 180 degrees and is facing the opposite way in hidari hanmi. As you do so drop the right hand, still in kamae position, so that it is hanging down by the side of your body. Don't use your strength to do this, and don't allow your hand to be too far forward or back.
③ Advance forward with the left foot in the same way as in (I), and come to a leaning-forward position. Keep both hands in the same position. Don't pull the right hand in toward you. The movement as done up to this point is the preparatory movement.
④–⑦ As you transfer your weight from your left foot to your right foot, keeping your weight over the toes of both feet, turn and face the other way. Together with the movement of

④　　　　　　　⑤　　　　　　　⑥

the upper body, bring your right hand up from its position by the side of your body in a circular movement, keeping it in line with your center of balance, so that it is raised to head height. Raise your left hand as well, making sure that it stays directly in front of your body, and bring it to nose height. Once you have finished the turning movement you should have raised the hands in the same position as in hiriki no yōsei ichi.

⑧–⑨ As you return and transfer your weight from right foot to left foot, cut down with both hands along the same path and return to the preparatory position. Return and repeat the movements.

IMPORTANT POINTS

● **Don't perform the movement in such a way that your center of balance stays between the front and back feet and you merely turn your body around.**
● **In the middle position of the movement, make sure that your weight stays over your toes.**
● **Do not wait until you have finished the turning movement to raise the hands. Make sure that you raise them as you are making the turning movement, taking care that your elbows do not get stuck too close in to your body.**
● **Make sure that your hips don't get left behind and that your body doesn't come to a twisted position.**
● **Without changing the height of your hips or knees, by transferring your balance in a horizontal movement you can keep your weight over the same line.**

Control the whole body as one unit

● Without changing the height of your hips or your knees, and by moving in a horizontal turning movement, you will be able to transfer your weight from one foot to the other while moving your center along the same line. You should not move away from this line—to the left or to the right—with either the upper or the lower body.

● The turn of the hips, knees, and ankles, together with the raising of the hands, should all take place in one movement in time with your breathing. This means that all parts of the movements should both start and finish together.
(The diagram below shows the movement of the whole body as seen from above).

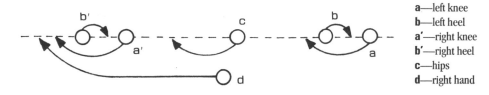

a—left knee
b—left heel
a′—right knee
b′—right heel
c—hips
d—right hand

TAI NO HENKŌ ICHI
BODY CHANGE MOVEMENT I

① ② ③

⑦ ⑧

IMPORTANT POINTS

● The leg and hips move together as they make an "S" movement. It is incorrect to do this movement with the foot alone.

● Both hands are kept in front of the body. As the hips change direction, the hands follow in a circular movement. The hands move as though the backs of them were following the surface of a ball.

● The whole body moves smoothly without a feeling of jerking at any stage.

● Having turned your wrist into the palm of uke's hand, change the direction of the movement without losing that power.

④ ⑤ ⑥

The hips move in a V shape, the basis of "body entry" (irimi).

This is the method of training the body movement when being pulled. In one smooth movement the hips move forward in a V shape, changing the line of power and causing uke to become powerless. By controlling your own hands, feet, and hips along one line, you can come to a stable posture. This movement of the feet and hips is the basis of the body entering movement (irimi) and is also directly connected to katate-mochi sokumen irimi-nage (one-hand grasp; side entering throw).

The same movement, shown from different angles, is introduced both for solo practice and for practice with a partner.

① From migi ai-hanmi kamae, uke grasps your left hand with his right hand, and pulls in a straight line.

② Blending with the pulling power, your left foot passes in front of your right foot in a circular movement, and the palms of your left and right hands face each other as they go forward.

③ Sliding the left foot forward in a circular movement, change the direction of your hips to the left. The palms of both your hands are facing up, with the left hand at head height and the right hand at chest height.

④–⑤ Keeping the upper body in that position, bring your left foot forward in a large movement, keeping the balance forward. When working with a partner, your left hand enters into the left of uke's neck with a circular movement, your right hand comes palm up along the side of uke's body. Your left foot moves forward between uke's feet.

⑥–⑧ When coming back on the return movement, slide back your left foot in a big movement, and at the end slide your right foot in so that you return to the original position. Repeat the above movements.

TAI NO HENKŌ NI
BODY CHANGE MOVEMENT II
Redirect the energy by making a 95-degree turning movement

① ② ③

This is the method of redirecting power when being pushed. This movement enables us to make a turning movement "tenkan" while maintaining a stable posture, so that by keeping the balance over the same foot and making a turning movement to the rear, we can unbalance the other person. Many unbalancing techniques develop from tai no henkō ni.

① From hidari gyaku-hanmi kamae, uke grasps your left hand and pushes in a straight line.
②–④ Blending with the pushing power, keep the balance over your left foot and make a 95-degree turn to the rear with your right foot. At the same time bring your left hand around in a scooping movement so that it comes to chest height with the palm facing upward. The right hand is turned in the same way as the left hand, and is brought up to hip height.

Uke's Position
Pivoting around the point where you had grasped, your elbow is bent inward, and your power is redirected forward in a circular movement.
⑤–⑧ Return along the same path so that you come back to your original position. Repeat the movement.

IMPORTANT POINTS
● Keep your energy flowing forward as you make the turn, and drop your weight straight down over the front foot.
● In order not to bring your balance backward, make sure that you turn with the feeling of turning forward.
● When you make the turn, make sure that you keep your hands, hips, and feet on the same line, and don't allow the different parts of your body to get out of alignment.
● When you turn the hands, keep them on the line that extends forward from the hips. Don't do the movement just by pulling in with the hands.

④ ⑤ ⑥

Keep your wrist fixed to the palm of uke's hand

When we say "Turn your hand around in a scooping movement," we mean that you should turn the wrist over in such a way that uke's four fingers, starting with the little finger, are caught up in the turn. By doing the movement in this way you can make a real connection with uke's power. Because uke has pushed in a straight line and can no longer release himself from the point where he gripped, his elbow is bent inward.

COMMON MISTAKES
● **You lose your center of balance and your weight falls backward.**
● **You pull your hand to the side and therefore lose your own correct posture.**

SHŪMATSU DŌSA ICHI
AFTER-CLASS EXERCISE I

①

②

③

⑥

⑦

⑧

This is a combination movement designed to teach us to harmonize our energy with our partner.

④ ⑤

⑨ ⑩

This technique is called "after-class exercise" because at the end of training we do it to stretch the body out. Originally, its purpose was to teach us to move from one position to another while maintaining a stable posture. By doing it in one continuous movement with a partner, it also teaches us to be sensitive to the other person's energy.

Shumatsu dōsa ichi is directly connected to ryōte-mochi shihō-nage (I). (Two-hand grasp; four direction throw I).

① From migi ai-hanmi kamae, uke grasps your wrists and pulls.

②–③ You move forward and to the right from the front foot, and changing the direction of the pulling power, bring both hands up so that they are extended in front of the chest. Hold the hands in a circular shape as though the palms were holding the surface of a ball, and make sure that you don't open up your elbows to the side.

④–⑤ Moving parallel to the line you were originally facing, make a large step forward with the left foot, and as you bring your weight over that foot, bring your hands up in a circular movement to the front of your head.

⑥–⑦ Keeping your weight over the toes of both feet, transfer your weight from your left foot to your right foot in the same way as in hiriki no yosei ni, and as you turn your body slide the left leg forward. Both of your hands stay in the same position as in the previous movement, and the arms extend straight up into the air.

Uke's Position

Keeping your left hand holding sh'te's right hand, allow your body to turn and slide up in time with the movement of sh'te's back, and hold on to Sh'te's right hand with both of your hands in a position behind your head.

⑧–⑨ As you move forward in a big step with your right foot, keep your hands in the extended position and cut down with them to shoulder height, and bring your balance strongly over the front foot.

Uke's Position

In time with sh'te's forward movement, move to the side, keeping your grip on his right hand, and allow your body to be bent back.

⑩ As you bring up the back foot, return to migi-hanmi kamae. If you are working with a partner, take correct distance (*ma-ai*) and face each other.

IMPORTANT POINTS

● **In ⑦, the distance between the feet after you have made the turn is the same as in kamae.**

● **As you are making moves ⑤–⑨, make sure that you are not pulled off-line because uke is holding you. Uke, as well, should make sure that he does not pull sh'te toward him.**

SHŪMATSU DŌSA NI
AFTER-CLASS EXERCISE II
Raise the hand as you make a turning movement to the rear.

This exercise is to teach us to make continuous movements without interrupting the flow of energy, so that when somebody grabs both hands and pushes, we are able to make a turning movement to the rear, thereby changing the direction of the power and unbalancing the other person.

① From hidari gyaku-hanmi kamae, uke grasps both your wrists, and pushes in a straight line.

②–③ Keeping the balance over the left foot, make a 180-degree turning movement to the rear, slide your right hand up on the inside of uke's left wrist and raise the hand in a circular movement to head height. Bring the left hand around to chest height in a palm-up position, in the same way as in tai no henkō ni (Body-Change Movement II). Bring your body to a low posture, and extend the back leg strongly.

④ ⑤ ⑥

Uke's Position

The elbow of the right arm should be bent inward, the elbow of the left arm should be led around and up, and you should be brought off-balance with a feeling as though you were moving around the outside of sh'te's turn.

④–⑤ Keeping your balance over the toes of both feet, transfer your weight from your left foot to your right foot and change the direction you are facing, and bring your left foot forward so that you are in kamae position. Raise both hands straight above the head, without losing the extension of the elbows. The hands are held shoulder-width apart.

⑧ Slide forward in a large step with the right leg and bring your balance strongly over the front foot, coming to a low stance. At the same time cut down with both hands to shoulder height.

⑦ Bring the back foot forward and come to migi-hanmi kamae. If you perform the movement with a partner, take correct distance (*ma-ai*) and face each other.

IMPORTANT POINTS

● **When you are making the turning movement, make sure that you do not pull your hands into yourself. Apply the control around the circumference of the turning movement of your hips.**

● **Once you have finished the turning movement, both hands should be centered along your front line. Don't allow them to come off-line to the left or right.**

KIHON DŌSA
BASIC MOVEMENTS: IMPORTANT POINTS

When you are training in the basic movements, there are certain points that are vital for you to observe. As well as being applicable to actual techniques, it is also important to observe these points in all of the movements.

Open the fingers strongly

By opening the fingers, it is easy to extend power forward. It might appear that by making a strong fist and trying to control the arm in that way we would be very powerful, but actually in this position the power of the arm is flowing in toward us. If we extend our arm and allow uke to try to bend it, it is therefore quite simple for him to do that (picture ①). If, however, we strongly open the fingers, our power is being transferred forward, and it is much harder for uke to bend our arm than when we held our hand in a fist (picture ②). So if uke grabs your wrist, open up your fingers to make it difficult for him to grab you strongly, and to make it easier for you to take advan-

Bringing up the back leg

When you are making a movement to go forward, if you come to a position where your balance continues to extend forward, you will be able to develop strong power. In order to achieve this, once the leg that has advanced forward is fixed to the mat, continue to direct the energy of the knee forward. If you leave the back leg where it is and the forward power is stopped, you will not be able to extend power. It is also important, in order to keep a stable posture, to maintain the correct distance between your feet. Therefore, when moving forward in a movement, as you extend forward with your front knee make sure that you slide your back leg up.

It is also important when you are moving forward that the back foot is attached strongly to the mat, so make sure that the back knee is strongly extended and that the surface of the foot is flat against the mat—do not allow your

Your whole body moves as one unit

When you are moving, if one part of your body is too fast or too slow, you will not have one line of power and thus will not be able to develop shūchū-ryoku. Therefore it is important to move in such a way that all the parts of your body move together, as in hiriki no yōsei ichi (figure A).
a) Raising both hands, b) pushing forward with the hips, c) moving forward at the knee, d) moving forward with the front foot, e) pushing back from the back foot—if all of the above are done together you will be able to create a single flow of power, and shūchū-ryoku will be developed.
In ③, as the balance comes over the front foot the front knee pushes forward, and the back foot slides up.
In hiriki no yōsei ni, where we transfer the weight from one foot to the other, or tai no henkō ni, where we make a tenkan (turning movement), if all the parts of the body

tage of the contact of his grip. When you make a strike, open the fingers to generate a lot of power.

In order to develop this ability, you have to pay attention to opening your fingers strongly when you are training. In the beginning, most people use too much strength when they try to open the fingers, but as you continue in your training, you will find that you are able to hold the fingers open naturally. When you open the fingers, you must make sure that your spirit is also being sent strongly forward.

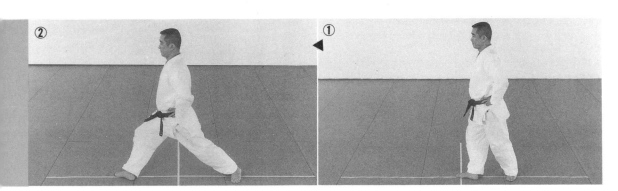

heel to "float." In this way you will be able to move forward without raising and lowering your balance.

move together, the hips and the hands are always facing directly along the body's front line. If the body becomes twisted the whole of the body's timing will be lost.

figure A

SHIKKŌ-HŌ
KNEE WALKING

Pull up the back heel

We use knee walking when doing a technique from a kneeling position so that we can move smoothly without losing our balance. Make sure that your hips don't float up; also make sure that you don't do the opposite and leave your hips behind by using just your feet to move with.

① Come to seiza (kneeling position) and stand up on your toes.
②–③ Keeping your balance over the right knee, move forward with the left knee as though pushing forward with the hips. As you do this pull your right heel forward, so that the heels of both feet do not become separated.
④–⑦ Once the balance is over the left knee move forward with the right knee and bring the left heel next to the right heel. Make sure that your weight doesn't fall to the rear, and that your balance moves forward with the front knee. By repeating these movements you will move forward.

IMPORTANT POINTS

● Make sure that your hips don't "float" and that your balance doesn't go up and down as you move.
● Keep your body straight above the hips, and don't move from side to side.
● Make sure that the front knee—the knee that is moving forward—does not come inside so that it crosses the center line of the body.
● When you have finished each part of the movement, your body will be in a "half-on" position, but make sure that the main line is straight forward.
● In order to move backward, pull the heels backward in a circular movement.

COMMON MISTAKES

Leaving your back heel behind, or turning your hips forward or to the rear are common mistakes. Make sure that both of your heels stay underneath your hips.

Turning movement

When you want to make a turning movement from a kneeling position, bring your balance over one of your knees and turn your body around. Both heels come around as though chasing the movement of the hips. Make sure that as you turn you don't "float up" with the hips and therefore break your posture.

UKEMI
FALLING

Forward rolling fall

Forward jumping roll

Fall to the rear

To prevent injury when thrown

The throwing techniques of aikido include simple throws as well as techniques where a twist is added. The art of falling not only enables you to escape injury, it allows you to move quickly to the next attack. Whichever fall you do, in order not to hit your head, your eyes must be looking at the knot in your belt the whole time. The following falls are representative but in reality, depending on the situation, you adapt to the circumstances in order to protect your body. By taking these falls in training, you will be developing strength and flexibility in your whole body.

● This is the basic method of rolling forward

① Have the same side hand and foot forward, and turn the hand so that tegatana is facing forward.
②–③ Turn your head to the side, and make the fall so that the whole line—from the hand through to the outside of the arm—comes into contact with the mat, all travelling along the same line.
④–⑤ The other hand lies next to your hip in preparation, and as the spine comes into contact with the mat, slap the mat with that hand. Don't turn your body to the side; the body moves along the same line right to the end.
⑥ Using your left foot as a fulcrum, use the momentum of the roll to stand up.

● You can be thrown from different angles, and this fall is useful for many of those throws. It is specially useful if you are thrown fast, or if the throw has had a twist added.

①–② Move straight forward with the front foot and bring your head in to your center. The other hand is held ready to slap the mat.
③ Make a high jump forward, and turn your body over as you are in the air.
④–⑤ Slap the mat with your hand so that all of your arm up to the shoulder hits the mat. Allow your body to make a circular roll along the mat, and pull your left foot right up into your hips. Make sure that your body doesn't become unbalanced and end up in a diagonal line.
⑥ With your left foot as a fulcrum, use the momentum of the roll to stand up.

● This is the fall that you would use if you were thrown backward and to the side, for example for shōmen irimi-nage and similar techniques.

① If you are thrown backward and to the right, pull your right leg back in that direction.
②–③ Drop your hips down so that they are close to your right foot, keep your left foot extended, and turn your body around to the right. Your right hand is held ready to slap the mat.
④ As your right hand slaps the mat, bring both feet around so that your body is lying straight.
⑤–⑧ As you come around to the right, your body is facing the other way from the direction in which you started.

SHŌMEN-UCHI
FRONT STRIKE

Transfer the power of your hips into your hand

In the same way that you would make a front strike with a sword, use your tegatana to make a strike to your opponent's head. By moving forward, the power developed by extending your balance forward can be transferred into your hand.

①–② When you come to a distance where your fingers would be meeting your partner's fingers if he extended his arm, raise your hand straight up above the center line of your body. Don't lift up your shoulders or open your armpits.

③–④ Pushing straight forward with your hips, strike with tegatana to your partner's face. Bring your balance strongly over your front foot. Push forward with your front knee to transfer the power of the hips into the hand. In one breath, bring your balance forward and strike.

⑤ This is shōmen-uchi as seen from the front. It is made with the hands, feet, and hips in one straight line.

IMPORTANT POINTS
● By spreading your fingers correctly you will extend your power forward.
● Don't raise your shoulders, and don't use only the power of your arm to make the strike.
● By bringing your back foot up at the moment of the strike you ensure that your posture remains stable.

COMMON MISTAKE
If you open your armpits, you will be unbalanced to the front. Because this will prevent you from pushing your balance correctly forward, you will not be able to transfer any power into your hand.

SHŌMEN-UCHI NO UKEKATA
BLOCKING THE FRONT STRIKE

At the moment that you make the block, turn your hand over

This is the method of protecting yourself against shōmen-uchi. It is not just a matter of stopping the strike: by turning your hand over at the moment that you make contact you will break uke's power and also bring your own body into a strong posture.

①–② From hidari gyaku-hanmi, uke takes one step forward with the front foot and attacks with shōmen-uchi. You harmonize with uke's strike, raising your hands.

③ As though pushing forward with the lower part of the right tegatana, block uke's strike. By using the hips and keeping the balance forward through the front knee, and extending strongly through the back leg, you will come to an immovable posture. Don't do this just with the arm, but have the feeling that you are performing the block with the hips. In addition, don't wait to block, but use your timing to block at the moment before the power enters uke's hand. Your left hand grips uke's elbow lightly from the outside.

● In aikido we block with the ulna, the forearm bone that is on the outside of the wrist.

How to blend with the wrists

①–② Do not merely hit each other in a straight line, but at the moment that you make contact with your partner turn

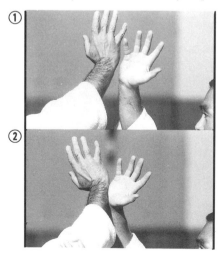

your hand over as in ②, so that you have the feeling of pushing forward with your wrist and elbow. By doing this you can neutralize the power of the strike without losing the flow of power. Open your fingers strongly. (Sh'te's hand is on the right).

COMMON MISTAKES

● If you block with your hand in a sideways position, you will not be able to stop uke's power.

● If you don't bring your balance strongly forward, your posture will be weak and you will be pushed back by uke's power.

SHŌMEN-UCHI NO UCHIYOKE
ENTERING INSIDE THE FRONT STRIKE
(FRONT STRIKE INSIDE-BLOCK)

Maintain the point of contact and lead your partner

As opposed to the block where you stop uke's power, this is the method where you take away the power of uke's strike and redirect the flow of energy.

①–② From migi ai-hanmi kamae, blend with uke's shōmen-uchi and move to the inside with the right foot.

③–④ While uke's hand is still at a high position, blend with your right hand (i.e., bring your hands into contact with each other).

⑤–⑦ Keep your weight over your right foot and make a 180-degree turn to the rear, and without losing contact with uke's hand turn your hand over so that the thumb is pointing downward. With a circular movement make a flowing block along your own front line. You should have the feeling of using your own hand to lead the power of uke's hand.

IMPORTANT POINTS
● If you pull the hand directly in toward yourself, the flow of energy will be interrupted and you will not be able to lead uke around. You should lead him around in a spiral movement along the extension of the line of the original strike.
● All of this should be done as one movement without stopping the flow of energy.
● While you are making the turn, make sure that your balance does not fall backward.

YOKOMEN-UCHI
SIDE STRIKE TO THE HEAD

① ② ③ ④

By turning your hips cut down along the diagonal

Strike with the hand by cutting down in a diagonal line, aiming at the area from the temple to the neck.

①—② In migi-hanmi kamae, raise your right hand straight above you in the same way as in shōmen-uchi.

③—④ As you move forward from the front foot, keep your elbow pointing forward and strike down in a diagonal line with the right tegatana. Don't merely lift your arm up to the side, but change the direction of the hips in order to change the direction of the cut. In the same way as in shōmen-uchi, bring your balance strongly forward over your front knee to transfer power into your hand. Open your fingers strongly in order to develop as much power as possible.

Where the strike should be made.

COMMON MISTAKES
● Make sure that you don't open your elbow to the side as you raise your hand, and also that you don't swing your hand around in a horizontal line as you make the cut.
● The hips should not be facing straight to the front.

YOKOMEN-UCHI NO UKEKATA
BLOCKING THE SIDE STRIKE TO THE HEAD

Control the strike the moment before it becomes powerful

This is the method of protecting yourself against yokomen-uchi. Rather than just stopping the strike, this is a method of controlling uke at the moment before his strike becomes powerful.

①–② From hidari gyaku-hanmi kamae, harmonizing with uke as he raises his hands, raise both your hands straight up.

③–⑤ Harmonizing with uke's strike, move forward along the diagonal line with the left foot, and cut down with your hands, using the front part of the left arm to make the block. At the moment that you make contact

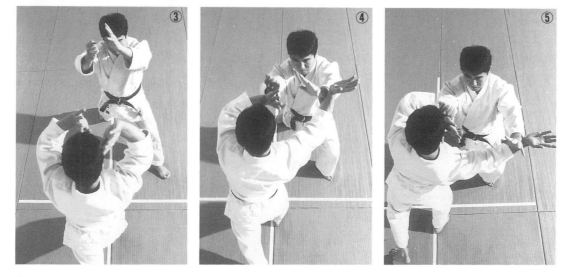

with your partner, turn your hand over to the outside in the same way as in shōmen-uchi. Use your timing to apply the block at the very moment before uke's strike

becomes powerful. At the same time the right hand makes a fist, and gives atemi to uke's face.

IMPORTANT POINTS
● When you move out to the side, make sure that you don't move on a straight line, and keep your own front line facing uke, with your face looking straight at him.
● Don't make the block just with your hands—use your whole body, and make sure that by bringing your balance strongly forward through the front knee you maintain a strong posture.

COMMON MISTAKES
● Don't open up your armpits, and don't strike with the hand by pushing from the inside to the outside line, otherwise you will be overcome by uke's power.
● Don't let your body face outward.

YOKOMEN-UCHI NO UCHIYOKE
ENTERING INSIDE THE SIDE STRIKE TO THE HEAD
(SIDE STRIKE TO THE HEAD; INSIDE BLOCK)

Cut down with the hand in a spiral movement

In the same way as shōmen-uchi no uchiyoke, this method takes away uke's power and redirects the flow of energy.

①–② From migi ai-hanmi kamae, harmonize with uke's strike: as you raise your right hand step forward and to the inside with the right foot.

③–⑧ Keep your balance over your right foot and make a turning movement to the rear. As you cut down with your left hand make a flowing block, re-directing uke's strike along a spiral line. The flow of power from uke's yokomen-uchi is maintained within this turning movement. At the same time, make a fist with the other hand and deliver an atemi to uke's face.

⑦ This is the moment that you make contact with your partner, as seen from the opposite side.

IMPORTANT POINTS

● Don't just push down on uke's hand from above. Lower your stance at the same time as you make the turn, and the power developed by lowering your posture will automatically be transferred into your hand.

● Don't try to push uke's hand around, but after your hands have made contact trust the circular movement of your own body to lead it around.

● Make sure that your balance doesn't fall back as you make the turn. Keep your weight over one point right till the end.

SHŌMEN-TSUKI FRONT PUNCH

Push the knee forward and extend the power into the fist

The effectiveness of shōmen-tsuki is developed by pushing the balance forward and transferring that energy into the fist. Even if you were to punch in the correct manner but the front foot that had stepped forward was too stiff, the flow of energy would stop there. If the hips continue to travel forward even after the front foot is planted on the ground, as the hips push the balance forward, so your power is also pushed forward. By combining that movement with the punch, all of the power will be transferred into the fist. In order to achieve this, the knee must continue to push forward even after you have finished making the step. However, merely straining with the knee will not make the technique work. Training in the hiriki no yōsei (Elbow Power) basic movements will enable you to develop the necessary flexibility in the knees.

We will here give the explanation of a shōmen-tsuki in which the same-side hand and foot are both moving forward, but when the hand and the opposite foot are forward ("gyaku tsuki"), the principles are the same.

①–② From migi ai-hanmi kamae, pull the right foot back and pull the right fist in to the side of the body. Drop your weight straight down over the left foot.

③–④ As though you are pushing forward from the hips, move forward in a big step with the right foot, and punch in to your partner's solar plexus. The movement of the lower half of the body should be ahead of the movement of the upper part of the body.

⑤ Even after the right foot has been planted into the mat, continue to push forward with the knee and the hips, and bring your weight strongly over the front foot. This action should be coordinated with the punch to form one movement. The fist should be closed lightly at first, becoming tight at the moment of impact. The back foot should slide up naturally with the forward movement of the body, and the back leg should be strongly extended in order to give the body a stable posture.

IMPORTANT POINTS

● The hips must be held so that they are facing straight forward.

● Keep the fist in the center line of the body as you punch. Your hands, feet, and hips should all be on the same line, which will give you a stable posture.

● Don't tense the upper body (especially the shoulders), and don't use only the power of the arms to make the punch.

If you were to punch to kyūsho, a pressure point, using the single point of the second knuckle of either your first or middle finger would be effective.

MAKING A FLOWING BLOCK TO SHŌMEN-TSUKI

Move your own center line away from the line of the punch

When you are making a flowing block to a punch, if you try to escape with your body you will not be able to enter in. Avoid the punch by bringing your own body close to your partner, not to "escape," but to go the least possible distance in moving your own center line away from the line of the punch.

Outside flowing block

① Come to hidari gyaku-hanmi kamae. Uke pulls back the right foot one step and comes to the preparatory punching position.

②–③ Harmonizing with your partner's punch, maintain the feeling of moving forward as you keep your balance over your front foot and make a turning movement. Bring the left tegatana onto uke's forearm, and make a flowing block.

Ⓐ Because it is the movement of your body that brings your

own center line away from the line of the strike, there is no need to make a big step to the side to "escape" from the punch.

Uke's Position

To cause sh'te to come forward, make a punch to the front. At the moment that you put power into your fist to deliver the strike, your target disappears; the power of your punch continues to extend forward, and because the direction of the force is redirected, you are unbalanced in a big movement to your front.

IMPORTANT POINTS

● Although it appears that you are moving straight forward, by changing the direction of your hips, you are able to cause uke to miss his target. Even after you have avoided the punch, do not change your balance, which is over your front foot.

● Make sure that because of your desire to escape from the punch you do not distance your body from your partner's body.

Do not push uke's arm away with your tegatana, but rather make light contact, and by changing the direction of your own body redirect the line of energy.

Inside flowing block

① Come to migi ai-hanmi kamae. Uke pulls back one step with the right foot and comes to the preparatory punching position.

②–③ Keeping the balance over the right foot, make a big turning movement to the rear with the left foot and open up your body; bring the right tegatana to uke's forearm and redirect the power.

UNBALANCING YOUR PARTNER FROM KATATE-MOCHI (ONE-HAND GRASP) (WHEN YOU ARE BEING PULLED 1)

Control the little-finger side of the hand and turn the elbow over

This is the method of unbalancing your opponent when he has grabbed you in a position where his power is focused in his thumb. Because the power is centered in the thumb, the little-finger side of his hand will naturally be weaker, and it will be easy to open up his elbow to the side, so that is the direction we will go in order to control and unbalance him. Here we show you how to continue into kokyū-nage (breath throw) after you have made the unbalancing movement.

① From migi ai-hanmi kamae, uke grasps your left wrist with his right hand, and pulls in a straight line.

②–③ Blend with the pulling power, and keeping the balance over the right foot, make a turning movement to the side with the left foot, changing the direction of the body. At the same time, turn the hand that is being held so that it is in a palm-down position, and bring it around in a circular movement along the left-side diagonal line. There should be the feeling of bringing uke's palm around together with your wrist.

Uke's Position

As your pulling power is redirected in a circular line around to the right, your elbow is pushed backward, and you are unbalanced along the rear right-side diagonal line.

④–⑦ As you move forward with your right foot along the front right-side diagonal line, bring your left hand around in a circular movement as though turning the elbow around from the outside, and raise your hand to head height. This movement is not done in a straight line—turn your body to the left.

Raise your hand in such a way that the tegatana comes around the outside of uke's wrist.

Uke's Position

Because sh'te raises his hand, your elbow is also raised up, your shoulder is turned over, and you are unbalanced to your left.

⑧–⑪ As you move forward in a big step with the left foot and bring your body into a deep posture, cut down with your hand in such a way that your elbow stays at the front, and you turn uke's shoulder over and throw him.

IMPORTANT POINTS

● This technique should be performed with no break in the flow of energy.

● At the time that you change the direction of power, maintain your own stable posture and do not become unbalanced.

Atemi / The method of striking

Raise the hand through correct use of the elbow

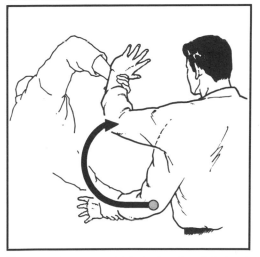

If you use just your wrist to try to raise uke's hand, you will find it difficult. Relax your wrist in the position that uke is holding it in, and raise your hand by keeping the wrist in your center and raising your elbow. As you raise your hand, your fingers will be pointing toward your head.

In a real application, if you use atemi at the same time as you unbalance uke, it becomes easy to move into the next stage of the technique, In addition, in applying atemi we cause uke to block, and thus prevent him from using that hand to hit us.

(WHEN YOU ARE BEING PULLED 2)

Cut your partner's elbow in to the inside

This is the method of unbalancing your partner when he has grabbed you and focused his power into the little-finger side of his hand, which has made his thumb side become weak. His energy is such that it is easy to turn his elbow in to the inside, so that is the direction in which we apply the lock, and thus we unbalance him.

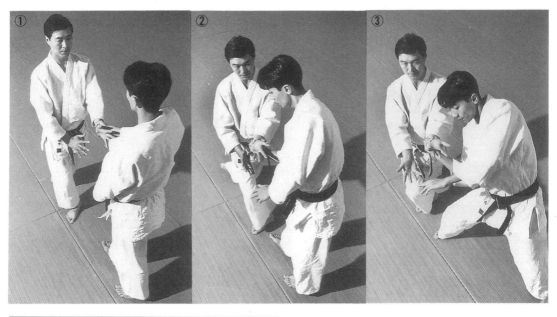

Change the direction of power by correct use of the hips

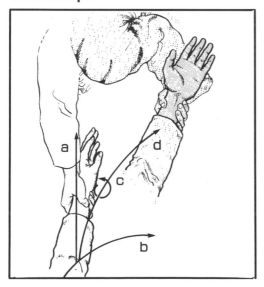

If uke tries to pull you in a straight line, then his power is moving along line a. As you move forward without trying

① From migi ai-hanmi kamae, uke grasps your left wrist with his right hand, and pulls in a straight line.

②–③ Blending with the pulling power, bring your right foot up to uke's right foot so that they meet in a T-shape, and change the direction of your hips. Bring your balance strongly over the right foot and come into a low posture. At the same time, turn your left hand so that it is palm up and push it out at chest height.

Uke's Position

As the line of power is changed so that your hand comes into a palm-up position, your elbow is cut in to the inside (toward the hips) and you are unbalanced.

to resist that pull, change the direction of your hips so that they are moving along line b. At the same time, extend your arm out along line c, turning the hand palm up. The line of power has now been changed to line d, and uke's elbow has been brought in to the inside line. Make sure that you change the direction of the line of power by changing the direction of the hips, not merely by raising your hands to the side. Your hand has to stay in the center line of your body.

UNBALANCING YOUR PARTNER FROM KATATE-MOCHI (ONE-HAND GRASP) (WHEN YOU ARE BEING PUSHED 1)

Keeping the center over uke's front foot, turn the power in a circular movement

This is a method of unbalancing your partner when he has grasped your hand, focusing his power in his thumb. When you are pulled, you use uke's energy to unbalance him, but when you are pushed, you redirect the flow of energy. The control is applied in the direction of the weak point, the little finger.

① From hidari gyaku-hanmi kamae, uke grasps your left wrist with his right hand, focusing his power into his thumb, and pushes in a straight line.

②–④ Blending with the pushing power, move to the left side with the left foot, and at the same time extend the left hand forward in a circular movement along the left front diagonal line, turning the hand so that the palm is face down. Do this movement in such a way that the palm of uke's hand does not get separated from your own wrist.

Uke's Position

Keep your focus on your front foot, where you already had your weight. As your pushing power is brought around in a circle to your right, your body is extended and unbalanced.

⑤–⑥ Keeping your weight over your front foot, as you make a large turning movement with your right foot to the rear, bring your left hand up in a circular movement to head height, turning over Uke's elbow and shoulder.

(WHEN YOU ARE BEING PUSHED 2)

Moving the hand in order to release the grasp

This is a method of redirecting the energy when uke has grabbed your hand and is pushing, focusing his power into the little-finger side of his hand. Here we will show you how to release your hand from the grasp by using tai no henkō ni. You would make the same movement with the hand if you were being pulled.

① Using the turning movement of tai no henkō ni, redirect uke's pushing power.

②–③ Having turned the palm of your hand up in a scooping movement during (1), now turn the hand so that the palm is face down, and release your hand between uke's thumb and first finger. At the same time bring your right tegatana from underneath uke's hand.

④ At the moment that you release your hand from uke's grasp, use the back of your right hand to redirect the energy. This control or technique should be done as one continuous movement as you are making the turn.

UNBALANCING YOUR PARTNER FROM KATA-MOCHI (SHOULDER GRASP)

From kata-mochi, as from katate-mochi, the direction in which you unbalance uke depends on which method he uses to hold you. Here we will show you how to bring your partner "up," from a position where he is pulling you.

From a position where the back of uke's grasping hand faces up

① From migi ai-hanmi kamae, uke turns his right hand so that the back of the hand is facing upward, and holds the front of the shoulder of your dōgi (as though holding a piece of paper), and pulls. In this position, the power is focused in his thumb and first finger, so the control is directed to the little finger.

②–③ Blending with the pulling power, move forward and to the left in a circular movement with the left foot, and at the same time extend forward in a circular movement with your left hand along the front left-side diagonal line, turning the hand over so that it is palm down. As you apply this control, the left shoulder moves so as to fix itself to uke's fist. Make sure that your own front line is always facing toward uke.

Uke's Position

As your pulling power is redirected, your elbow is pushed behind you so that you are unbalanced, and at the same time the movement of sh'te's shoulder locks up your wrist.

④ Using your right hand to fix uke's fist to your shoulder, as you move forward and to the right raise your left hand up so that you slide uke's elbow into the air. As you apply this control together with the movement of the shoulder, the little-finger side of uke's hand that is holding you will be turned over, and his elbow will rise in the air.

From a position where the palm of uke's hand is turned inward

① From migi ai-hanmi kamae, uke turns the palm of his hand to the inside, grabs the front of the shoulder of your dōgi by folding his fingers in starting from the little finger, and pulls. Uke's power is focused into the little finger in this position, so the control will be applied against the thumb. Rest the inside of your forearm against the outside of uke's elbow.

②–③ As you turn the toes of your right foot to the outside, move forward so that your foot meets uke's front foot in a T-shape, and as you move your hips to the right, extend your hands forward and turn them palm up. As you apply this control move your left shoulder so that the direction of uke's hand is changed and his elbow is turned inward. Your left hand moves in order to hold the position in place. Make sure that you do not use just your arm to give a push.

USHIRO WAZA HOJŌ DŌSA PREPARATION MOVEMENTS FOR ATTACKS FROM BEHIND

We use the some preparatory movements for all attacks from behind. In this example, we show ushiro ryōte-mochi (Two-Hand Grasp from Behind).

① – ③ From migi ai-hanmi kamae, uke attacks with shōmen-uchi. Sh'te turns his right hand up and blocks, at the some-time bringing his left hand back to the side of his body, ready for the next strike.

④ With the left fist, sh'te gives a punch into uke's solar plexus (stomach).

⑤ – ⑧ As uke moves forward, he uses his hand to cut sh'te's arm down and runs around behind sh'te's back.

⑨ From his position behind sh'te's back, uke grasps both wrists. (Shoulder, elbow, or collar grasp is done in the same way).

All of the above movements are part of the basic technique. In advanced techniques, we can use the action of uke running behind us as part of the technique.

UNBALANCING YOUR PARTNER FROM USHIRO RYŌTE-MOCHI (TWO-HAND GRASP FROM BEHIND) (WHEN YOU ARE BEING PULLED)

① Uke grasps both of your wrists from behind, and pulls in a straight line. Your hands remain slightly in front of the side of your hips as they are held. If you allow your hands to get behind this line, you will lose to uke's power.

② Blending with the pulling power, bring your left foot to the left side in a circular movement, and change the direction of your hips. At the same time drop your weight down, and drop down with your wrists, so that uke's hands have only a light grip on your wrists.

③–⑤ Raise both hands up in front of you in an egg-shaped movement, causing uke to "float." Don't open your arms up too far to the side or try to turn your wrists over too quickly.

Uke's Position

Once you have been brought to the position where you cannot put any power into your hands, as sh'te raises his arms gradually come back to the position where you are holding his wrists in the palms of your hands, so that at the end of the movement, at the point where sh'te has raised his hands, you can again hold on strongly.

Once you have completely "floated" uke, you can then change position and apply the throw. Cut down in a circular movement with both hands so that your thumbs are pointing downward.

UNBALANCING YOUR PARTNER FROM USHIRO RYŌTE-MOCHI (TWO-HAND GRASP FROM BEHIND) (WHEN YOU ARE BEING PUSHED)

① Uke attacks from the rear, grasping both wrists and pushing. Keep both of your hands slightly in front of the hips.

②–③ Blending with the pushing power, as you move forward with the right foot, allow the hips to sink down and drop both wrists down. Make sure that you don't just pull forward on your own, so that you become separated from uke.

Uke's Position

As your pushing power is taken forward, you come to a position—in the same way as in pulling—where you cannot put any power into your hands.

④–⑧ Starting with the fingers, raise both hands in the air in front of your body in an egg-shaped movement, so that uke's elbows are "floating."

UNBALANCING YOUR PARTNER FROM USHIRO RYŌKATA-MOCHI (BOTH-SHOULDER GRASP FROM BEHIND) (WHEN YOU ARE BEING PULLED)

(When you are being pulled)

① Uke comes from behind and grasps your shoulders in a finger grip, and pulls.

②–④ Blending with the pulling energy and keeping the balance over the right foot, pull your left foot back and to the left in a circular movement and change the direction of your body. At the same time, turning your hands over so that the palms face outward, turn your elbows over in a small move-

ment. By combining this control with the movement of the shoulder you can change the line of power of uke's pull, and come to a position where Uke is "riding" on top of your shoulders.

Uke's Position

Because of the movement of sh'te's shoulders, your hands are turned to the inside, and so the pulling power that was going upward has now been redirected downward.

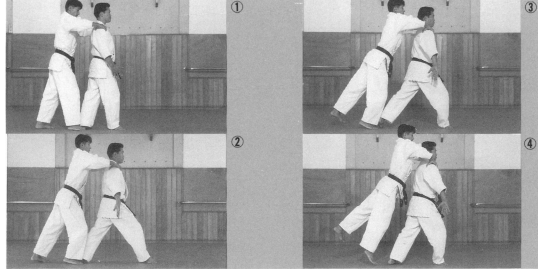

(When you are being pushed)

① Uke comes from behind and grasps your shoulders in a finger-grip, and pushes.

②–④ Blending with the pushing power, as you move forward with the right foot, turn both elbows forward. In the same way as when you were pulled, don't allow them to get behind you, but keep both elbows by the side of your body and then turn them. Your hands should move from a palm-in

position to a palm-out position. By use of this control, your shoulders become narrower as you move forward, and Uke's elbows are raised up.

Uke's Position

As your pushing power is taken forward, you are unbalanced to the front and your elbows are raised up, so that the line of the original pushing power is changed from upward to downward.

UNBALANCING YOUR PARTNER FROM USHIRO RYŌHIJI-MOCHI (BOTH-ELBOW GRASP FROM BEHIND)

(When you are being pulled)

① Uke attacks from behind, grasping your elbows in a fingergrip, and pulls.

②–④ Blending with the pulling power, turn your hands from a palm-in position to a palm-out position. At the same time turn your body slightly to the right, and pull the front foot in. Bring your elbows into strong contact with uke's palms, and move your energy right through to uke's elbows.

Uke's Position

As sh'te turns his elbows over in a circular movement, your pulling power is redirected and sh'te's power comes into your elbows: your elbows are raised up, you are extended onto your toes and become unbalanced.

(When you are being pushed)

① Uke attacks from behind, grasping your elbows in a fingergrip, and pushes.

②–④ Blending with the pushing power, move forward with the right foot and turn your elbows over to the front. Your elbows should be slightly further in front of you than in the pulling position.

Uke's Position

As sh'te turns his elbows over your pushing power is taken forward: your hands are pointing inward, your elbows are brought up, and as you "float" you are unbalanced.

KIHON WAZA / BASIC TECHNIQUES

Everyone,
You may think "How should this technique be done," "How should that technique be done,"
But the thing to remember is, although there are many techniques,
You must grasp the principles that underlie them.
It comes down to shifting your balance quickly,
Moving your hands, feet, and hips as one.
The basis of it is shihō-nage.
As Ueshiba Sensei said, "To throw to the four directions, this is the essence of aikido.
Therefore, shihō-nage on its own, if performed correctly, is sufficient."
This is what he taught.

—— Gozo Shioda Sayings (III) ——

WHAT DO WE LEARN FROM BASIC TECHNIQUE TRAINING?

Basic techniques teach us to redirect uke's attacking power, to unbalance uke by maintaining the flow of energy without interruption, and they build in us the ability to perform the more advanced techniques.

For example, let us have a look at shōmen-tsuki kote-gaeshi ni (front punch; return-the-wrist throw II).

①–③ As you make a blending block with uke's shōmen-tsuki, turn your body and then move forward. In this way, you can lead the power of uke's punch and unbalance him forward.

④ Before uke can regain his balance, keep your weight over your front foot and make a turn to the rear, at the same time turning uke's hand over in the kotegaeshi position. Uke will again be brought forward by the movement.

⑤–⑥ As you make another turn in the same direction, cut down with the right wrist and make the throw.

As you will understand by looking at the above technique, once you have unbalanced your partner, you can lead him around without allowing him to regain his balance, and then you can apply the technique. That is why we do repeated training of these body movements, until they are fixed deep in the body, in order that we can then perform the basic techniques.

However, if you just monotonously repeat the movements, so that actually you are making up your own body movements, there is no meaning to the training in basic techniques. We must be ever-faithful to the basic movements, training with the objective of understanding how to lead the energy in the correct direction and how to develop correct power in our own bodies.

SHIHŌ-NAGE
FOUR-DIRECTION THROW
Containing the basics of all of the throwing techniques

In shihō-nage, by making a circular movement with your own body, you fold your partner's arm over his shoulder and, as though cutting downward with a sword, throw him to the rear.

Depending on uke's attack and the way you use your body, you can throw uke to any of the four (or eight) directions, which is how this technique got its name.

In order to be able to throw uke to any of the four directions, blend with his energy and without stopping that extension lead him to the direction in which you intend to

throw him, coming to the point at which his body is both extended and cut down. Because this body movement contains all of the basic principles of aikido, shihō-nage can be seen as expressing the root of all of the aikido throwing techniques, and as such is given extreme importance in training.

Since the attacker's elbow and shoulder are locked out as he is thrown, shihō-nage is very effective as a self-defense technique.

Use against multiple attackers

Because with this technique you can throw in any direction, it is particularly effective against multiple attackers. For example, if you were to throw the first attacker in the direction of the second attacker who was coming toward you, you could use him as a screen to block that attack.

KATATE-MOCHI SHIHŌ-NAGE ICHI
ONE-HAND GRASP; FOUR-DIRECTION THROW I
METHOD OF GRASPING THE WRIST

By locking out his wrist and elbow, you cause uke's body to "float."

①–③ From migi ai-hanmi kamae, uke grabs your left wrist and pulls in a straight line. You strike with a right-handed back-fist atemi to uke's face.

④–⑤ Harmonizing with the pulling power, advance your

right foot along the forward diagonal, extend left hand in a circular movement with the palm down directly in front of your body, and with your right hand hold uke's right wrist.

⑥–⑦ As your left foot comes forward in a big movement, both hands cut up in a circular movement to forehead height, and the front knee is focused strongly forward.

▼

Uke's Position

Because of the control being exerted by sh'te's left hand, by the completion of the first movement (⑤), your right wrist is bent back so that the elbow is extended (straightened), and your body is "floating."

At the completion of the second movement ⑦, because of sh'te's upward cutting action, your elbow is bent inward and your body is extended forward.

⑧–⑩ Change direction and shift the balance of the body in the same way as in shūmatsu dōsa. Cut down with both hands to chest level, cutting uke's hand down over his shoulder blade. As you change direction pull the back (left) foot forward. Hold uke's wrist from the inside, and straighten your own wrist so that the first finger is pointed forward. Without losing the extension of the elbow, be slightly relaxed as you maintain your hold. Keep your left hand in the lower position.

Uke's Position

Because your body starts from an extended position, it is not possible to stand up as your arm is bent back, and you have to take a step backwards to maintain balance.

⑪–⑫ As you move forward from the front foot, drop your body down and throw uke to the rear. Drop forward with your whole body, keeping your arm fixed in its position—rather than pulling in with your arm—to unbalance uke. As uke falls, bring your right hand down beside your right ankle.

⑬ Bring your weight strongly over your right foot and as you lock uke's wrist down, raise your left hand and strike to his face with tegatana.

IMPORTANT POINTS

● To lead uke to the point at which you can fold his arm over and back, you must focus on his shoulder when you move his arm.

● After you have changed direction and shifted your balance ⑨, if the hand that is cutting down (the one holding uke's wrist) is higher than chest height, you will not take uke far enough back to break his balance.

● Hold both hands normally in the front of the body.

● The last strike with tegatana should be made with the some spirit as a samurai on the battlefield finishing off his enemy. Uke uses his left hand to protect the face.

Changing the Direction of Power

Pull your little finger into uke's wrist, and have your thumb lying against his pulse.
(Changing the Direction of Power)
The hand that is pulled cuts through uke's hara (center).

① In katate-mochi shihō-nage, turn uke's wrist with the first movement. As you move forward with your whole body, the back of your left hand makes firm contact with uke's palm, so that there is no gap between the two hands.

② Harmonizing with the pulling power, move to the front right-side diagonal and turn the left wrist over so it is palm down; at the same time the tegatana makes an arc, in order to apply the control. The feeling is of tegatana cutting horizontally through uke's hara. If it is done correctly, uke's hand will be bent back, and it will be as though he is being carried along on your hand.

③ As you move forward in this position, uke's elbow is extended and his shoulder is pushed up, so that he "floats."

Method of grasping the wrist

Bring your right hand up so that it crosses over your left hand, and grasp uke's wrist.

COMMON MISTAKE
Don't come to a position where you are underneath uke's hand. Both when you raise uke's hand and when you cut down, have the feeling of raising and cutting down with the sword.

How to fold the arm over

Cut as though with a sword

In turning uke's arm over, you must have the feeling of cutting down with a sword, as you change stance and shift your balance.

① Once you have raised your hands, make sure that uke's body is extended.
② It is important that, as you change direction, both of your hands are held naturally in front of your head. This will ensure that when uke's arm is bent, his elbow is folded inward, and he is not able to regain balance. With the movement of your left hand you can change the direction of uke's arm.

③—④ Cut down by extending your arm in front of you. Don't cut down only on uke's elbow; by focusing on his shoulder as you move behind him, you take his arm and the whole of his body with you.

KATATE-MOCHI SHIHŌ-NAGE NI
ONE-HAND GRASP; FOUR-DIRECTION THROW II

Change the line of the pushing power, and bring the elbow inward

① From hidari gyaku-hanmi kamae, uke grabs your left hand and pushes. You strike to uke's face with a right-handed back-fist atemi.

②—④ Pivoting on the left foot, make a 180-degree turn to the rear. At the same time, blending with uke's pushing power, bring your left hand up in a circular movement to head height, and with your right hand grasp uke's wrist in the same way as in katate-mochi shihō-nage ichi.

⑤—⑧ As you shift your balance and change the direction of your body, pull your back (left) leg further forward bend uke's arm over his shoulder blade. The right hand is at chest height.

⑦—⑧ As the right leg goes forward, drop the whole body down and throw uke to the rear. The left tegatana then cuts down to uke's face.

IMPORTANT POINT
● At the same time as you are making the turning movement and raising your hands, his elbow is bent inward, and his whole body becomes extended.

YOKOMEN-UCHI SHIHŌ-NAGE ICHI
SIDE STRIKE TO THE HEAD; FOUR-DIRECTION
THROW I

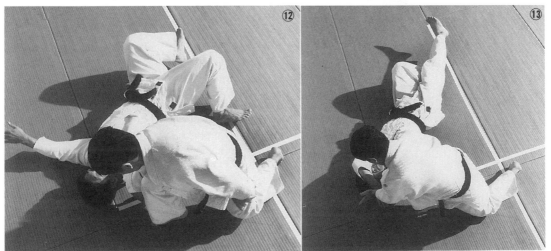

Control uke's palm and raise your hands.

①–② From migi ai-hanmi kamae uke raises his hands ready to strike, and you raise your own hands at the same time.

③–⑤ Pivoting on the front (right) foot, make a large turning movement to the rear. Enter inside uke's yokomen-uchi, and block smoothly. The left hand blocks and cuts down to chest height, the right hand gives a back-fist atemi to the face.

⑥–⑦ As the front (right) foot opens up along the right-handed front diagonal, slide your left hand down until it reaches the bone just above uke's thumb. Your right hand holds onto the back of uke's right hand from over the top, with the thumb lying over uke's wrist as though taking his pulse.

⑧ As the left foot moves in a big step forward, slightly on the left-hand front diagonal, in a circular movement bring the

hand that you are holding up to head height.

⑨–⑩ As you shift balance and change the direction of your body, with a movement as though cutting down with a sword, cut down with uke's arm so that it comes over his shoulder blade.

⑪–⑫ As you step forward with your right foot, drop your body down and throw uke to the rear.

⑬ Finish the technique by striking down with the left tegatana.

IMPORTANT POINTS

● In ⑧, bring your hands up so that uke's palm is facing toward you. By doing this you ensure that the elbow will be facing inward, and you will be able to take away his balance.

● The movements in pictures ⑥–⑧ should make a V-shape when progressing forward and to the side.

● When making a turning movement, make sure that your balance doesn't go backwards. Similarly, when moving to the side, make sure that your balance is firmly over the front foot.

HANMI-HANDACHI RYŌTE-MOCHI SHIHŌ-NAGE
ONE SITTING, ONE STANDING; TWO-HAND GRASP; FOUR-DIRECTION THROW

Changing from high to low, cut down the arm

This technique does not have I, II classification

① You are in seiza. Uke approaches from the front, grasps both of your wrists, and attempts to pull them up.

②–③ Blending with the pulling energy, bring the left knee up, advancing one-third of the length between uke's feet, and pull the right knee forward. At the same time make a horizontal cutting movement with the left hand, as in katate-mochi shihō-nage ichi. With the right hand grasp uke's right wrist.

④–⑤ Continue to move forward with the left foot (advancing the same distance as in the first movement) and stand up, bringing the back foot in so that the feet are in kamae. Keep-

ing the hands in the same position, raise them to head height.

⑥–⑧ Pivoting on the left foot, slide the right foot behind you, changing direction; at the same time drop your body lower and cut uke's arm over his shoulder blade.

⑨–⑩ Moving forward with the right leg, drop your body and throw uke to the rear.

⑪–⑫ Keeping your balance strongly over the right foot, continue to cut down on uke's arm. With the left tegatana, strike down to uke's face.

IMPORTANT POINT
● **To cut down uke's arm, use the power that comes when you drop from the standing position to the final kneeling position.**

79

SHŌMEN-UCHI SHIHŌ-NAGE KUZUSHI
FRONT STRIKE; FOUR-DIRECTION THROW
EXTENSION (PRACTICAL APPLICATION)

Change direction without changing your balance

①–② As uke attacks with shōmen-uchi, raise your hand high so that your and uke's tegatana meet.

③–④ Keeping the balance over the right foot as you make a big turning movement to the rear, come to the inside of uke's strike and make a smooth block.

⑤–⑦ The right foot opens up onto the right-side diagonal, and the left foot steps in. Bring the left hand to the bone just above uke's thumb, and grasp uke's wrist with your right hand. At the same time, as you raise both hands, pivot on the right foot and change the direction of your body. (Do not allow the weight to transfer to the left foot as you pivot.)

⑧–⑩ As you make a big step forward with the right foot, cut down to the front with your right hand, and throw uke.

IMPORTANT POINT

● ⑤ As your body opens up to the side, move forward so that your hands (holding uke's wrist) make a big arc in front of your hara. You will thus be able to lead uke's power in a spiral, and you will be able to use the spiralling movement to raise your hands.

IKKAJŌ
FIRST CONTROL

Bring uke to a prone position by turning over his elbow

Ikkajō is a technique in which by turning over your partner's elbow you are able to bring him to a prone position.
This ikkajō movement is the basic method of turning the
elbow over as used in other techniques from nikajō onward.

Taking uke to the ground and applying pressure by pushing down on his elbow is called the ikkajō pin.

Beginners find it difficult to apply pressure directly downward from a seiza position, but it is only through techniques such as this that the true power of aikido, i.e.,
using the focused power of the whole body, can be learned.
Just as it might be said that *budō* in its highest form can
be found in the basics, so it could be said that ikkajō is
the most basic of techniques and also the most difficult.

If we turn uke's elbow over and throw him instead of taking him to the ground, the technique becomes ikkajō-nage.

THE MECHANICS OF THE IKKAJŌ PIN

SIDE-VIEW

FRONT-VIEW

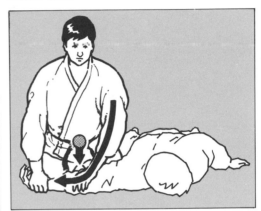

Open out uke's arm to at least 90 degrees

Having brought uke to the prone position, open out his arm so that it is at least 90 degrees to the spine. That makes it difficult for him to put power into his arm, and his resistance is decreased. Of course, his elbow must be completely turned over.

Dropping the weight of the whole body, make the pin

(Preparatory Position) Once you have brought

uke to the prone position, bring your knees down so that one knee is on the inside of the hand that is gripping uke's wrist, and one knee is inside his armpit. Be on your toes. Using this control, stretch uke's arm completely.

(Pinning Technique) Bring the palm of your hand over the top of uke's elbow, as though enveloping it up. Straighten your back, breathe out deeply, and with a feeling of pushing your lower stomach into the mat, drop the whole of your body down, allowing the weight to come into uke's elbow. Allow the weight to come directly into his arm, but also allow the power to flow right through to his fingertips. Don't bend your elbow or drop your head.

Straining with your upper body will cause your hips to "float"

It is easy to bend your back and use your shoulders in an attempt to push all of your weight into your partners elbow if you do not understand the feeling of "applying the lock by using your hips." The effort, by straining with your upper body, will cause your hips to float and for you to lean over. The result is power not being transferred into your partner. In this connection, you should not apply your power to one point in the elbow; rather, control your energy so that it penetrates into the elbow.

COMMON MISTAKE

SHŌMEN-UCHI IKKAJŌ OSAE ICHI
FRONT STRIKE; FIRST CONTROL I

Change the direction of the energy and turn the shoulder over

①—③ From migi ai-hanmi kamae, you (sh'te) attack with shōmen-uchi. The purpose of this strike is to cause uke to block. As uke blocks, grasp under his elbow with your left hand.

④—⑧ As your right foot goes forward on the front right-hand diagonal, use your right tegatana to cut down in a circular movement. The left hand assists in this movement as it turns uke's elbow over. With your balance centered strongly over your front (right) foot, you will control uke's elbow and shoulder. As you cut down with the right hand, grasp uke's wrist. (Do not grasp the wrist at the beginning of the movement.)

Uke's Position

As the power in your blocking arm is redirected, the elbow and shoulder are turned over in a big movement. At the same time, your body is turned around.

⑦—⑧ Your left foot advances along the front left-side diagonal, and you unbalance uke to the left, as though pushing his

arm through the shoulder. In this position your body should be in a low posture.

⑨—⑪ As your right foot advances, move the left knee into uke's armpit, and bring uke to a completely prone position.

⑫ Lower your right knee, and pin the elbow.

COMMON MISTAKE
If you try simply to twist uke's arm, his shoulder will be unaffected and you will not be able to turn his body around. The basic principle of this technique is to project the technique into the shoulder and control uke at the moment he strikes.

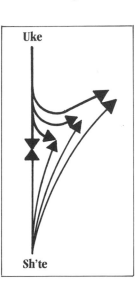

How to change the direction of the power

At the moment the arms come together, the power of both sides is coming straight on and therefore they clash. If you turn your tegatana to the outside and at the same time change the direction of your body and move forward, the power which is coming from uke will be taken over by this circular movement and will be redirected. Uke's elbow will also be turned over.

Uke

Sh'te

SHŌMEN-UCHI IKKAJŌ OSAE NI
FRONT STRIKE; FIRST CONTROL II

Leading the other person around in a spiral

①–② Come to hidari gyaku-hanmi kamae. When uke strikes with shōmen-uchi, block with your right tegatana and with your left hand grasp his elbow.

③–⑤ As you turn uke's hand smoothly to the right and turn his elbow over, pivot on the toes of the left foot and make a 180-degree turn to the rear. As you are making the turn, lower your posture, and make sure that uke's elbow is in

front of you, so that the distance between you doesn't change. Without having the feeling of pulling, you should be using both arms on the same line as the hips are turning, the upper and the lower body moving as one. Your body should not come to a twisted position. Once you have moved uke far enough around, grasp his wrist.

⑥–⑨ When you have made the 180-degree turn, transfer your weight from the left foot to the right foot in the same way as in hiriki no yōsei ni. Drop the body and pull the left foot into uke's armpit. This changing of balance causes uke's

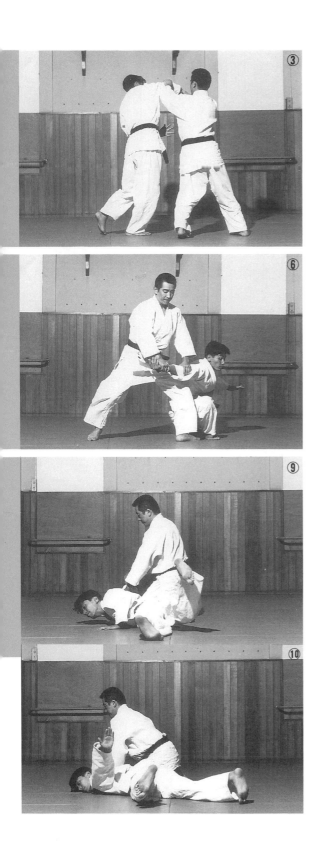

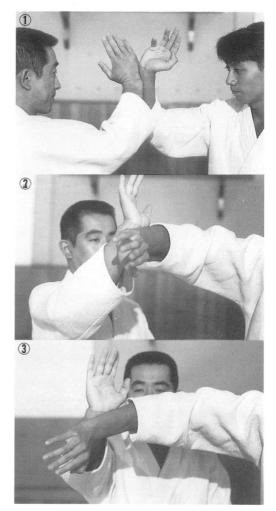

Redirecting the flow of the attacking energy

① When you receive the front strike, the power is still coming straight at you.

② As you change the direction of your body and turn your right tegatana over, you redirect uke's power to the right.

③ As you come around in the circular movement, uke's elbow will turn over.

body to accelerate and together with the turning movement rolls him over. Both your hands should be using equal strength, without any feeling of pushing uke's elbow or pulling in on his wrist. As you complete the turn bring your left knee to the mat. The steps from ④ to ⑩ all happen in one movement, and lead uke around in a spiral.

Uke's Position

The power from shōmen-uchi is directed around to the left, your elbow and shoulder are turned over, and you are pulled around in the circular movement.

⑩ Lower your right knee and pin uke's elbow.

SUWARI WAZA KATATE-MOCHI IKKAJŌ OSAE ICHI / KNEELING TECHNIQUE: ONE-HAND GRASP; FIRST CONTROL I

By manipulating your own elbow, turn over uke's elbow

①–② Come together and kneel in seiza. Uke holds your left wrist with his right hand and pulls in a straight line. Blending with the pulling energy, move across to the left and, keeping the left hand in a palm-down position, extend it out to the front left-side diagonal, changing the direction of the pulling power and unbalancing uke. At the same time, make a back-handed atemi to his face with your right hand.

③ Using shikkō (knee walking), move sightly forward along the right-side front diagonal. Maintaining uke's hold, bring your left hand up in a circular movement in front of your face. With your right hand, hold onto the back of uke's right hand, fixing it to your left hand.

④–⑤ As you take a big step with your right knee along the front right-side diagonal using shikkō, cut your left tegatana

down in a circular movement as though pushing uke's elbow in front of you, causing uke to be unbalanced.

⑥ As you take another small step forward with your right knee, free your left hand by pushing the left wrist forward, releasing it from uke's hand. It is possible to cut uke's hand too far forward, so to prevent this keep a good grip with your right hand.

⑦–⑨ As your left hand slides down to uke's elbow, in the same way as in the standing technique move forward with the left knee and then the right knee in the direction of uke's left armpit, bringing uke to a completely prone position. The left knee is in uke's armpit, and the right knee is to the inside of your own right hand which is holding uke's wrist. Keeping his wrist fixed, pin the elbow.

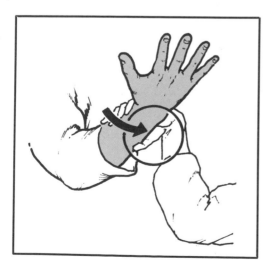

Sh'te's tegatana attacks the point at which uke's thumb is attached to his hand

The tegatana turns inside the hand that is holding it, and attacks the point at which the thumb is attached to the hand.

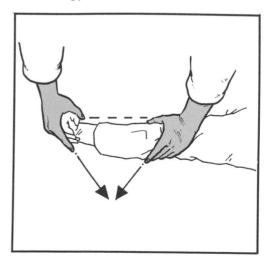

Ikkajō lock on the wrist

Apply the lock as though bringing together the index fingers of both hands in a triangular position. When you bring uke to the mat, make sure that his wrist is turned strongly to the front.

KATA-MOCHI IKKAJŌ OSAE NI SHOULDER GRASP; FIRST CONTROL II

By controlling the shoulder, turn the elbow over

①—③ From hidari gyaku-hanmi kamae, uke grasps your left shoulder and pushes. As you move away to the left side, bring your left hand round in a circle to the front-left side diagonal, keeping the hand palm down, redirecting the line of power and unbalancing uke. (Uke's knuckles should now be fixed to your shoulder.) At the same time, make a back-handed atemi to his face with your right hand.

④—⑧ Bring your right hand over uke's right hand and fix it to your shoulder. Pivoting on the left foot, make a 45-degree turn to the rear and slide your left arm up raising uke's elbow in the air. At the same time use the movement of your left shoulder to turn uke's hand over. Do not use your left hand to push the elbow up. The left shoulder, which controls the wrist and turns it over, causes the elbow to "float,"

⑦–⑪ With a feeling as though you are pushing the elbow forward in front of you, pivot on your left foot and make a 180-degree turn, and then shift your balance, cutting down with the left tegatana in a spiral movement, bringing uke to a prone position. Again it is the movement of your left shoulder that turns over uke's grasping hand, together with the cutting down of your hand. Don't use the strength of your arms to try to merely push uke's hand away.

⑫ Release uke's hand from your shoulder, drop your right knee, fix uke's hand, and pin the elbow.

Fixing uke's hand to your shoulder

The purpose of fixing uke's hand to your shoulder is so that the shoulder/hand can act as a fulcrum in turning the elbow over. This fulcrum should not change until the end of the movement. From this position, by correct usage of your own shoulder, you can turn uke's hand over while keeping your thumb underneath, causing his elbow to "float." (Pictures ④–⑧).

USHIRO RYŌTE-MOCHI IKKAJŌ OSAE ICHI

Turn uke's elbow over by controlling his upper and lower body

①–③ The entry into this position is explained in 'Preparation Movements'. Change the direction of the power pulling on both wrists from behind. Raise both hands in a circular movement as though in the shape of an egg, causing Uke's elbows to rise up.

④–⑧ Keep the left foot still, and pull the right foot back in a 180-degree turn, bringing the body to a low posture and dropping the hands, with the thumbs pointed downward, to in front of the chest. The feeling is of dropping the whole weight of the body directly over the left foot. If in this position the weight of your body goes backward, pulling uke into you, you will not be able to unbalance him in a forward direction. Also make sure that you make a big turn so that you are not standing on a parallel line with uke.

Uke's Position

From the raised position of ④, your power goes from high to low. As your wrist is being dropped to the front right-side diagonal, you make a big movement forward and your left shoulder is turned over.

⑦ Keeping the hips at the same height, bring the right foot up behind the left foot and grasp uke's left elbow from below with your right hand. Maintain your left hand in its position so that it does not move—this will keep uke in an off-balance position.

⑧–⑨ As the left foot takes a big step forward, make a scooping motion with your left hand so that you end up holding uke's wrist, and at the same time cut down with your right hand.

⑩–⑫ As the right foot and then the left foot move forward through the direction of uke's armpit, bring uke to a prone position, fix the wrist to the ground, and pin the elbow.

TWO-HAND GRASP FROM BEHIND; FIRST CONTROL I

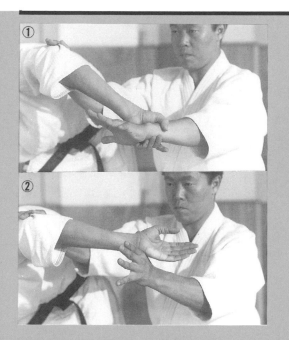

Gathering the wrist by scooping from below

As your right hand goes forward connected to uke's elbow, his left hand that is holding your wrist will naturally release its hold. Scoop up his wrist from below with your thumb and turn it over, then as you hold the back of his hand bend his wrist in.

USHIRO KATATE-ERI-MOCHI IKKAJŌ OSAE NI

As you turn, pull uke forward and around

①–③ Uke grabs your left wrist and the back of your collar from behind, and pushes. Blending with that power as you come forward, move away along the line of the push, and raise both hands in the air in the shape of an egg.

④–⑥ Pivoting on the right foot, turn the left foot 180 degrees around so that you are standing 45 degrees to the right in front of uke. Turn your left hand around inside uke's gripping hand, so that your tegatana is facing forward. Make sure that the balance is over the right foot. As you change direction, give a strike with the right fist to uke's armpit. The purpose of this strike is to make uke release his right hand from the grip it has behind your collar.

Uke's Position

As a result of sh'te's turn, your right hand, which is gripping his collar from behind, will be stretched out, and your left elbow will be turned over. Your body should be twisted around forward and to the right.

⑦–⑫ With your right hand hold onto uke's elbow, and extend your left tegatana around to the left. Pivoting on the right foot, make a 180-degree turn and then shift the balance (as in hiriki no yōsei ni), bring uke to a prone position, and pin the elbow.

WRIST AND COLLAR GRASP FROM BEHIND; FIRST CONTROL II

Using the tegatana when the wrist has been grasped

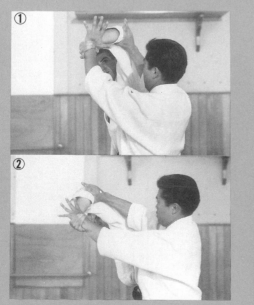

In this technique we utilize the hand that is grasping us right to the end. Keeping your elbow extended in kamae, turn the left tegatana around, with the feeling as though the wrist is entwined by uke's fingers, and in a spiral movement come around and down. As you are performing this movement, your hand will naturally grasp uke's wrist. As uke loses balance, his body will naturally follow the direction his wrist is going in.

95

NIKAJŌ
SECOND CONTROL

Turn the wrist over and drop uke's body to the ground

Nikajō is the technique whereby we turn uke's palm in the direction of the outside of his elbow, then cut down so that we destroy his posture. It is not a matter of merely twisting uke's wrist, you have to apply the technique so that his whole body sinks down. To achieve this, make both his wrist joint and his elbow joint into a V-shape and maintain that position as you cut down. This will ensure that uke's power is locked in his wrist, elbow, and shoulder, and as a result his body will drop down. Do not waste your power by merely turning uke's wrist around; it is important to understand the correct angle and line in order to unbalance uke.

Uke's tegatana should be vertical

If the position of uke's hand is not correct before you cut down, nikajō will not be effective. As in the picture, your right palm is attached firmly to the back of uke's hand, and your little finger is locked over his wrist. Your left hand is gripping the wrist lightly. Make sure that uke's tegatana is standing vertically, in front of your own center line, as if uke's hand was a sword that you were holding. Your tegatana should be turned toward uke's center line. If at this time you relax your hold on uke's hand, you will not be able to bend his wrist when the time comes to cut down.

Gripping method

Nikajō pin (lock)

①

Cut down straight, without twisting

Putting the lock on while holding with both hands

① As you turn over uke's wrist and fix it in position, you must be in a position along Uke's front diagonal line. If you stand directly in front, you will not be able to bend the elbow sufficiently as you turn it over.

② As you move forward from the front leg, cut the wrist down as though cutting through Uke's center line. As you do this make sure that you don't change the distance between the hand that you are holding and your own body. Keeping the upper body fixed in the same posture, move forward by focusing on pushing with your hips.

Also, make sure that you don't twist the wrist, otherwise the direction of the power will be wrong, and you will not be able to use the power that you develop by moving forward. Once you have brought the wrist into the second control position, maintain that shape right until the end.

③ Using the energy that you develop as you move forward, maintain the relationship as uke's body begins to sink down. Keep on the center line as you cut the wrist down to below your chest height, and have the feeling of moving along the line of uke's unbalance. You should have the feeling of cutting Uke's little finger down toward his nose.

COMMON MISTAKES
❶ Pulling uke's wrist toward you or, alternatively,
❷ Pushing uke's hand away from you.

Bring the palm of uke's hand face up, and lock his shoulder

The method of locking the arm once you have brought uke to a prone position is common to all nikajō osae techniques.

① Having fixed the wrist in second control position, bring uke to a prone position.

② Fix uke's elbow with your left hand. As you bring your right foot around to uke's foot, and your left foot under your hips so that you are looking across uke's shoulders, without changing the position of uke's shoulder, bring his arm around in the direction of his head, and bring the back of his hand to the inside of your left elbow.

③ With the inside of your left elbow grip uke's wrist with a scooping motion, and hold on to the front of your dōgi.

④ Bring up your right hand and fix it just below uke's elbow.

⑤ Cut your hips down toward uke's head, and lock his shoulder.

KATATE-MOCHI; NIKAJŌ OSAE ICHI
ONE-HAND GRASP; SECOND CONTROL I

Turning the elbow over

① Come to the position where you have locked uke's wrist in nikajō. As you move forward from here it is important not to grasp his elbow.

②–③ As you move forward along the front right-side diago-

nal and cut uke's wrist forward again, his elbow and shoulder will turn over. Make sure that you do not twist his wrist around to the right. Your left hand slides naturally down to the elbow and keeps the elbow and shoulder in position.

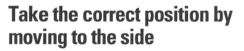

Take the correct position by moving to the side

① From migi ai-hanmi kamae, uke grasps your left hand with his right hand, and pulls.

② Blending with the power of the pull, pivot on the right foot, and bring your left foot around in a circular movement to the side. Your left hand comes around and forward in a circular movement, with the palm face down and held at hip height. By changing the direction of the pulling power you will unbalance uke. At the same time give a back-fist atemi with the right hand.

③–④ As you move slightly to the right with the front foot, scoop up uke's wrist between the thumb and forefinger of your left hand, and in a circular movement raise your hands in front of your face. Hold uke's right hand in nikajō position. You should be standing on uke's front right-side diagonal,

with uke's center line directly in front of you.

⑤–⑧ As your front foot moves forward, and you cut down uke's wrist toward his center, apply nikajō.

⑦ As you take one more big step with the front foot along your front right-side diagonal, apply pressure forward with the right hand and turn uke's elbow over. The left hand slides down to the elbow as you move forward, holding on in the same way as in ikkajō.

⑨–⑪ In the same manner as in ikkajō, bring the left foot and then the right foot forward in a big step through the direction of uke's armpit, and bring your left knee to the mat, bringing uke to a completely prone position.

⑫ Turning around uke's shoulder blade, change hands and apply the lock to the shoulder.

99

KATATE-MOCHI NIKAJŌ OSAE NI
ONE-HAND GRASP; SECOND CONTROL II

Turning the wrist over in front of you, lead uke in a circle

From hidari gyaku-hanmi kamae, uke grasps your right hand and pushes. Blend with the pushing power and move to the left from the front foot, bringing the left hand around in a circle, so that you move away from the line of the power, and unbalance uke. At the same time give a right-handed back-fist atemi to the face.

③ Pivoting on the front foot, make a 45-degree turn to the rear, and bring uke's wrist up in a scooping circular movement between your thumb and forefinger. Hold uke's hand in nikajō position in front of your face. You should be standing on uke's front right-side diagonal, with uke's center line directly in front of you.

④ As your front foot moves forward and you cut down uke's wrist toward his center, apply nikajō.

⑤—⑧ As the right hand continues to cut forward, and at the same time as uke's elbow and shoulder are turned over, pivot on the left foot and make a 180-degree turn to the rear. Without pulling uke's hand to the right, turn his elbow and shoulder over so that his body "floats," and lead him around in the turning movement. Make sure that uke's elbow always remains directly in front of you. The left hand slides down to the elbow as you are making the turn.

⑦—⑨ Without interrupting the momentum of the turning movement, transfer your weight from your left foot to your right foot in the same way as in hiriki no yōsei ni, and lower your hips. With the spiral shape of the turning movements, bring uke around and to a prone position.

⑩—⑪ Turn around Uke's shoulder blade, change both hands, and fix the shoulder, and apply the lock.

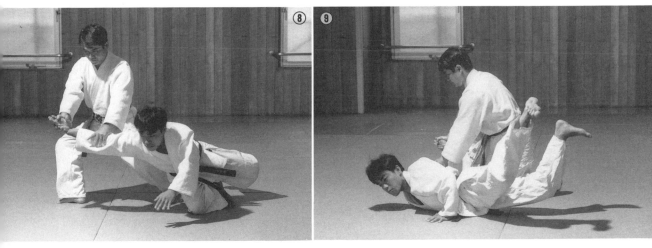

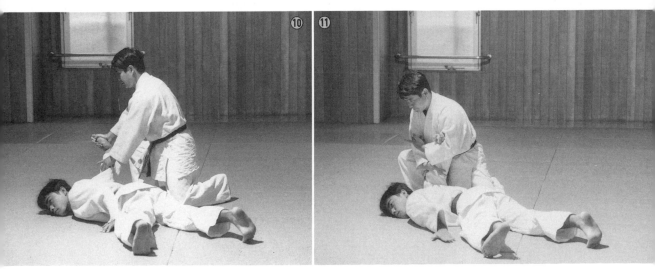

KATA-MOCHI NIKAJŌ OSAE NI
SHOULDER GRASP; SECOND CONTROL II

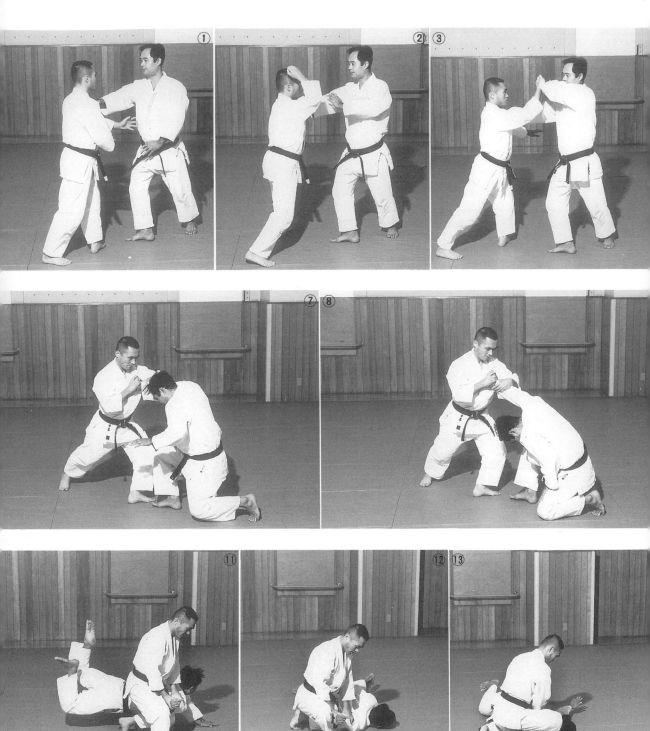

Apply the lock by pushing out the shoulder

①–③ From hidari gyaku-hanmi kamae, uke grips the shoulder of your dōgi, keeping the back of the hand uppermost, and pushes. Blending with the pushing energy, move sideways to the left from the front foot, changing the line of the power, and bring uke off-balance. At the same time, make a right-handed atemi with the back of the fist to uke's face.

④ Bring your right hand over the back of uke's left hand and grasp it, fixing the hand to your shoulder.

⑤ Pivoting on the left foot, make a 45-degree turn to the rear and use the inside of your left hand to slide uke's elbow up into the air. Together with this movement, use your shoulder to bring uke's hand into the nikajō position. You should

be standing on uke's front right-side diagonal, with uke's center line directly in front of you.

⑥–⑧ As you go forward with the left foot, slide the left hand down to uke's wrist, and push out your shoulder in order to bring on the nikajō lock. Do not use your hands to drop uke's hand down, but use your shoulder right until the end in order to make full use of the technique. Make sure that uke's thumb is fixed firmly to your shoulder. The lock should be applied in the direction of uke's center line.

⑨–⑫ Keeping uke's wrist fixed to the shoulder in the same position, start the turning movement. As uke's elbow and shoulder are turned over, slide your left hand down and hold his elbow. As you are making the turn, uke's hand will naturally come away from your shoulder.

⑬ Fix the shoulder and apply the lock.

SHŌMEN-UCHI NIKAJŌ OSAE NI FRONT STRIKE; SECOND CONTROL II

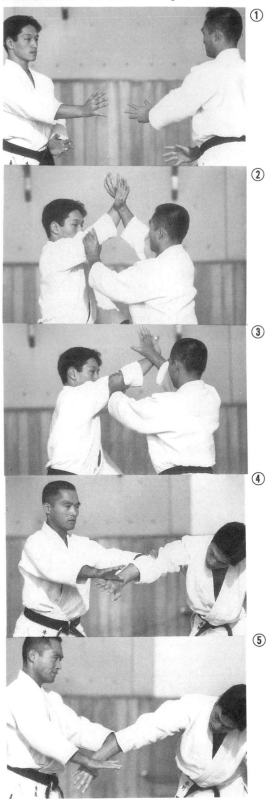

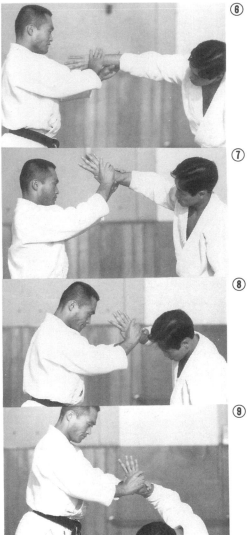

Explanation of the lock only

①–② From hidari gyaku-hanmi kamae, uke makes a shōmen-uchi with the right tegatana you block.

③–④ As you turn your tegatana to the right and redirect the line of power, pivot on the left foot to make a 180-degree turn. Cut your tegatana down to chest height in a spiralling movement. At this time make sure that the thumb is pointing downward and is placed on the outside of uke's wrist.

⑤–⑦ As you turn your body to the left, bring the right hand up in a big circular movement in front of the body, scooping up uke's wrist between the thumb and forefinger of your hand and holding it in nikajō position in front of your face.

⑧–⑨ From a position on uke's front right-side diagonal, cut down the wrist toward uke's center line, and lock it in nikajō.

HIJI-MOCHI NIKAJŌ OSAE ICHI
ELBOW HOLD; SECOND CONTROL I

①   ②   ③

④   ⑤   ⑥

Explanation of the lock only

① From migi ai-hanmi kamae, uke grasps the left elbow of your dōgi, grips it with the back of his hand facing up, and pulls. Blending with the pulling power, pivot on the right leg, moving the left leg around and to the left in a circular movement. At the same time, the left hand comes round and to the front in a circular movement, changing the direction of power and bringing uke off-balance. With the right hand give a back-fist atemi to the face.

② Bring your right hand over the back of uke's right hand and grip it, fixing it to your elbow.

③–④ As the right foot moves to the right and you change the direction of your hips, keeping the left tegatana facing inward slide your left elbow upward and bring uke's wrist to

nikajō position. Bring the elbow up so that it slides along the fold in the wrist underneath uke's tegatana. This movement is designed to prevent uke's hand from relaxing. At the end bring your elbow over the top so that it is resting on top of uke's wrist.

⑤–⑥ As you go forward from the front (right) leg, keep uke's elbow in the same position and cut down with tegatana toward uke's center line, turning your hand over as you do so, and apply nikajō lock. Make sure that uke's hand is fixed firmly to your elbow, as it is important that it can't move away as you are cutting down. Also, make sure that you don't drop the elbow. It is not a matter of lowering the elbow, but rather of changing the angle in order to lock uke's hand.

KATATE-AYAMOCHI NIKAJŌ UDEGARAMI-NAGE

Throw uke by rolling the wrist over

①–② From migi ai-hanmi kamae, point your right hand to the left side and offer it to uke. Uke comes in with his right hand to take your right hand (katate-ayamochi, Cross-Hand Grasp).

③–④ As your wrist is grasped, pivot on the front foot and make a 180-degree turn to the rear with the back foot. Blend with uke's incoming energy and lead it around.

⑤–⑦ Bring uke's hand around and raise it up through the direction of your finger-tips, and as you move forward from the front foot cut the hand down, applying nikajō lock.

⑧–⑩ Pivoting on the front (right) foot, open up the body 180 degrees, turn your right elbow around and turn your right wrist around to face to the inside. Bring the left hand over uke's elbow, locking out the upper arm, and bring his arm down in udegarami-nage.

CROSS-HAND GRASP; SECOND-CONTROL ARM-LOCK THROW (PRACTICAL APPLICATION)

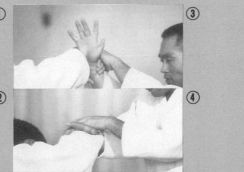

Nikajō locking method for ayamochi

① Keeping the fingers pointing inward, allow the wrist to be grabbed.

② Raise the hand as you bring it around in a circular movement in the direction of the fingertips. At the same time bring the body around in an evasion movement [tai sabaki] in the same direction as the hand, so that you come to a position on uke's front right-side diagonal.

③ As you come around to face uke, roll your wrist over so that tegatana is facing forward, and come into position for nikajō. The left hand comes from above to rest

on uke's hand, and fixes it. If you lose the connection between the hands the throw will no longer be effective, so make sure that the bend of your right wrist is fixed tightly into the joint of uke's wrist. Without straightening your arm, control uke's wrist so that there is no looseness there, and bring the fingertips around so that they are facing uke's center line.

④ As you move forward, keep your tegatana facing uke's center line, and cut down. Keeping uke's elbow fixed, turn the fingers downward, and turn your wrist around inside uke's hand as you adjust your grip. The purpose of this is to ensure that uke's elbow doesn't rise up.

SANKAJŌ
THIRD CONTROL

Unbalance uke by making him "float"

In the sankajō technique we unbalance uke by raising his elbow in the air and turning his wrist so that the back of his hand goes in the direction of his armpit. As opposed to nikajō, where we unbalance uke by making him drop down, in sankajō we create the unbalance by extending uke's body upward. It is not a matter of merely twisting uke's wrist—by bringing uke to a position in which he can no longer move his elbow or shoulder, we can control his whole body.

How to hold
Bring uke's arm to a U position

Before applying the control, raise uke's elbow in the air and grasp the back of his hand. In this position bring the lower three fingers around his tegatana, making sure not to grip with the thumb and forefinger. Bring uke's hand to an upright position by point-

ing your thumb and forefinger straight forward, with your elbow in kamae position. Bend the back of uke's hand around so that the elbow and shoulder are turned forward, and the arm forms a U shape.

COMMON MISTAKE

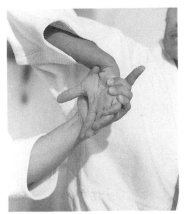

If you hold the wrist so that it is bent inward, sankajō will not be effective.

Applying the lock

Push uke's tegatana in a circular movement toward the armpit

An explanation of applying the lock using circular movement.

❶ Stand in hidari-hanmi kamae, to the right side of uke, and grasp his hand in sankajō position. Make sure that your own hand is in the center of your body.

❷–❸ Maintaining the shape of your own hand, pivot on the left foot and bring your body around in a circle of at least 90 degrees. By applying this control, you will bring uke's hand around toward his armpit.

Uke's Position

As your wrist is brought around toward the armpit your shoulder comes forward and the power of the lock enters it, so that your shoulder is raised up and the whole of your body "floats." Sh'te's turning movement also unbalances you, and you make a large movement to the rear.

❹ Keep your own hand in front of your body. When turning, it is your body movement that is most important. Make sure that you do not move your hand out to the side.

COMMON MISTAKES

If you attempt to twist uke's wrist around in too big a movement, your own hand will come to a flat (horizontal) position and you will only be turning his wrist—the lock will have no effect on his elbow or shoulder. Also, if you allow your own elbow to rise up, it will be difficult to apply the correct power.

Applying the pin

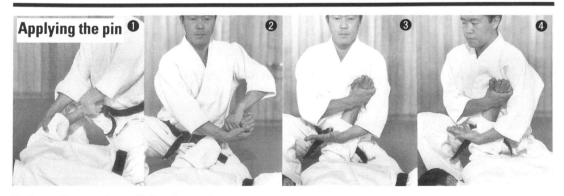

Bring the palm of the hand to your chest, and cut down with the hips

❶ Having applied sankajō, bring uke to a prone position.

❷ Without loosening the control, bring your body around so that it is facing across uke's shoulders. At the same time bring your right hand to your left hand and grasp the back of uke's hand in a scooping motion.

❸ Without loosening the control, bring your left hand away and transfer uke's hand into your right hand. Bring uke's palm to the left side of your chest, and fix it. At the same time, bring your left tegatana onto uke's elbow.

❹ With the feeling of pushing the palm of his hand with your chest, cut down with your hips toward uke's head and lock his shoulder.

YOKOMEN-UCHI SANKAJŌ OSAE ICHI
SIDE STRIKE TO THE HEAD; THIRD CONTROL I

By moving forward, lock out the elbow and shoulder

①–② From migi ai-hanmi kamae, uke aims a strike with his tegatana to your temple. Bring the left foot around in a circular movement to the side and turn out the left tegatana to block, simultaneously giving a right-handed back-fist atemi to uke's face.

③ Bring your right tegatana over so that you are scissoring uke's arm between your two hands in an X position.

④–⑤ As you move forward in a big movement with the right foot, use the right tegatana to redirect uke's power in a circular movement to the right. The left hand helps to redirect uke's power, and as uke's elbow is turned over, the left hand grasps it. In this position cut down and to the front with both hands, unbalancing uke and bringing him to the mat.

Uke's Position

When sh'te blocks, continue to apply force to cut down along the diagonal [toward Sh'te's temple]. As that force is redirected toward your left side, your elbow and shoulder will be turned over.

⑥ Slide your right hand down to uke's fingertips and, as though turning his hand inside out, turn it over and forward. At the same time take a small step forward with the right foot, turning uke's elbow and shoulder forward.

⑦ With your left hand grasp the back of uke's hand in preparation for sankajō.

⑧ As the left foot comes forward in the direction of uke's right shoulder blade, thrust forward with the left hand (which is holding uke's hand), and apply sankajō. The right hand grips uke's elbow, fixing the angle of the arm.

Uke's Position

As sankajō locks out your elbow and shoulder, and the power comes through toward your shoulder blade, you are unbalanced forward from the right shoulder.

⑨ As the right foot comes forward bring your body into a low posture, drop the left knee to the ground, and bring uke to a prone position.

⑩ Change position, fix the elbow, and apply the pin.

IMPORTANT POINTS

● **When you move forward as you are applying the sankajō, make sure that both of your hands stay on your own center line.**

● **When you apply the sankajō, make sure that uke's wrist is not turned inward.**

Turn uke's palm forward in a circular position

How to turn uke's hand over before applying sankajō

① Grip uke's four fingers just below the knuckle in a scissoring movement between your thumb and forefinger. This will prevent uke from closing his fist and thus make it easier to turn his wrist over.

②–③ Turn uke's hand over from the palm, so that the palm turns upward and ends up facing forward. With this control the whole of the arm should be bent like a bow and the shoulder turned forward.

YOKOMEN-UCHI SANKAJŌ OSAE NI
SIDE STRIKE TO THE HEAD; THIRD CONTROL II

Unbalance uke along the line of the arm's extension

①–③ From hidari gyaku-hanmi kamae, uke strikes with yokomen-uchi. Move to the left, turn the left tegatana out, and block. At the same time, give a right-handed back-fist atemi to the face.

④–⑤ As the right hand comes over in an X position, pivot on the front (left) foot and make a large turning movement to the rear, and redirect uke's arm around so that it comes to chest height.

⑥ With your right hand hold uke's fingers in the same way as in the I technique, and as you open up the front (left) foot to the side turn uke's wrist around and raise his elbow up in the air.

⑦–⑧ Take hold with the left hand in sankajō position, and pivoting on the left foot, bring the right foot around and forward in a movement of at least 90 degrees, and apply the lock. Your feet should be in left-handed kamae stance.

⑨–⑩ As you glide the left foot back behind you in a circular movement, cut down the left hand in a circular movement so that it comes to the side of your left hip, and as uke is pulled off-balance and toward you, give an atemi to the face with the right fist, keeping the back of the hand downward. As you bring the left foot behind you pull the right foot in slightly to ensure that the weight of your body doesn't go backward.

Uke's Position
Once the sankajō lock has been fixed (8), sh'te leads your arm in a circular movement along the extension of the line from the wrist to the elbow, and as your right shoulder turns over you are unbalanced downward. As a counter to sh'te's atemi, block with your left hand.

⑪–⑫ As your left foot slides backward and to the left, bring the four fingers of your right hand over the top of uke's elbow so that the fingers are pointing inward, and pull uke in toward his wrist. Make sure that your left hand doesn't loosen its grip in sankajō position. As you pull uke in slide the front foot so that the weight of your body doesn't fall backward.

Uke's Position
As your elbow is pulled around in a circular movement to the right, your shoulder follows, so that you end up in a low, off-balanced position in the direction of the elbow.

③ ④ ⑤

⑨ ⑩

⑪ ⑫

→✳ Photos continue on page 114

⑬ ⑭

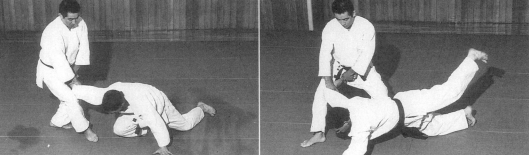

⑬–⑮ As uke becomes unbalanced, open up and move to the side from your right foot, bringing uke with you along the same line. Maintain the sankajō position in the same way as in the I technique. Bring the left knee to the ground and uke to a prone position.

Uke's Position

From the unbalanced position that you were in at the end of the previous move ⑫, as Sh'te locks out your shoulder and moves forward along the changed line, move forward with him and come to a prone position as you are brought to the ground from the right shoulder.

⑱ Change position, lock the shoulder, and apply the pin.

Bring the hand up so that you are looking at the palm

① Having redirected the power of yokomen-uchi, hold uke's fingers in the same way as in the I technique. At this time you should be standing to the side of uke.

②–③ Open up to the side from the front foot, turn and face toward uke's armpit, and raise uke's hand in a scooping motion.

You should end up holding uke's hand in front of your own face with the feeling as though you are looking at the palm of his hand. Do not squeeze uke's fingers, but have the feeling of raising his elbow by locking through the wrist. Make sure that his hand remains in front of your own center line. Your left hand comes to his elbow to prevent it from moving away.

④ Your left hand grips across the back of uke's hand, with your little finger hooked around the side of his hand. You must make sure that uke's hand is vertical, or the next part of the control will be weak.

⑤ Bringing the first finger and thumb so that they are pointing toward uke, extend your arm and, as you make a turning movement, apply sankajō.

SUWARI WAZA KATATE-MOCHI SANKAJŌ OSAE ICHI / KNEELING TECHNIQUE: ONE-HAND GRASP; THIRD CONTROL I

Use the power of uke's bent wrist straightening.

①–② Kneel in seiza, facing your partner. As uke grasps your left wrist and pulls in a straight line, blend with that power and bring your left knee around to the left in a circular movement, changing the line of power. At the same time give a back-fist atemi to the face with the right hand.
③ As you move forward slightly from the right knee, bring up your left hand in a circular movement to in front of your face, turning over uke's elbow, and with your right hand grasp the back of uke's hand.

④–⑤ As you take a large step forward from the right knee, cut down in a circular movement with tegatana, sending uke's elbow forward so that uke's elbow and shoulder are turned over.

⑥ As you take one more small step forward from the right knee, thrust the left hand forward, focusing on Uke's thumb (which is holding you), and release your hand from uke's grip. At the same time squeeze forward with the right hand, bending Uke's wrist.

⑦–⑧ As your left hand comes across and takes uke's wrist in sankajō position, with the left knee take a large step forward in the direction of uke's armpit, unbalancing him. Your right hand comes across and grasps his elbow.

⑨–⑩ As the right knee comes forward one more step, bring uke to a prone position, change your position, fix the shoulder, and apply the pin.

Changing the grip into sankajō

① Bend uke's wrist strongly forward, slide your left hand up inside your right hand, and grip the wrist.
② As you release with the right hand, uke's wrist will react to being bent forward by naturally returning to its original shape, and will come back into your left hand. At that point you can hold it in sankajō position.

USHIRO RYŌKATA-MOCHI SANKAJŌ OSAE ICHI
BOTH-SHOULDER GRASP FROM BEHIND; THIRD CONTROL I

As you turn uke's shoulder, shift your balance and apply the lock

Explanation of the lock

① Uke comes from behind and grasps both of your shoulders, and pulls.

② Blending with the pulling power, bring your left foot backward and around to the left, changing the direction of your body. At the same time bring your elbows around so that they are facing forward, changing the angle of your shoulders and making uke "float."

③–④ Pivoting on the left foot, bring the right foot around at least 180 degrees to the rear and drop your weight down. Keeping your left elbow extended to the outside, bring your arm to the center line of your body, and using the movement of your shoulder bring uke's left wrist to sankajō position. Your right hand grips the back of uke's hand and fixes it to the shoulder. Don't twist your upper body toward uke's armpit but rather, while keeping the upper body straight, drop your weight and bring the whole of the body to a low posture.

⑤–⑦ Transfer your weight from your left foot to your right foot as in hiriki no yōsei ni, bring the left tegatana so that it is pointing toward the inside, and at the same time, using the movement of the shoulder, apply sankajō.

USHIRO RYŌKATA-MOCHI SANKAJŌ-OSAE NI BOTH-ELBOW GRASP FROM BEHIND; THIRD CONTROL II

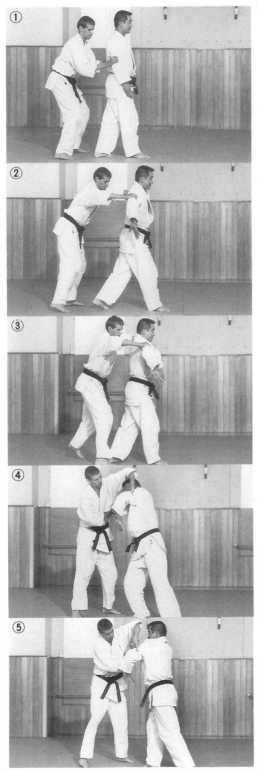

Apply the lock by turning your elbow over and making a turning movement

Explanation of the lock

① Uke grips both of your elbows from behind with his thumbs and fingers, and pushes.

②–③ Blending with the push, move forward with the right foot and turn your elbows forward in a circular movement, causing uke to "float."

④–⑤ Keeping your balance over your right foot, bring your left foot around in a circular movement of at least 180 degrees. As you do this, extend your left elbow out in front of you and bring it to your own center line. As you bring your arm around in this movement, uke's wrist will be brought into sankajō position. Grasp the back of uke's left hand with your right hand and apply the control with your left elbow. Do not twist around into uke's armpit, but raise his elbow; maintain a low posture to keep your upper body straight as you turn around.

⑥–⑦ Keeping you balance over your right foot, as you turn your body around to the right bring your left hang to the inside line, and together with this movement use your left elbow to apply the control.

YONKAJŌ
FOURTH CONTROL

In the yonkajō technique, we focus our power into our under-knuckle, where the forefinger is attached to the hand, and put pressure on the pulse point in uke's wrist, thus causing him intense pain. This pain causes uke to lose his ability to resist, and sh'te uses that situation to unbalance him. This is a technique that very simply shows the great effect that can be developed by concentrating all of the power of the body through one point.

Method of holding

The method of holding uke's hand, if you were to apply the technique to his right hand, is as follows: Turn uke's elbow and shoulder over and forward, and hold the back of his hand with your right hand. With your left hand hold uke's wrist so that the point where the first finger is attached to the hand comes inside the wrist. The little finger should hold on strongest, with each successive finger using less power. Straighten out your thumb and first finger. Hold on so that the palm of your hand is enveloping uke's wrist, not pushing it away.

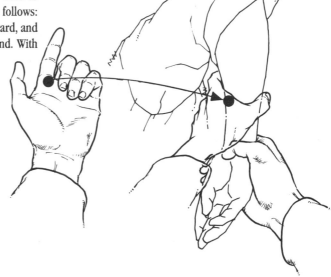

Method of locking

Using the principles of leverage, push the elbow forward

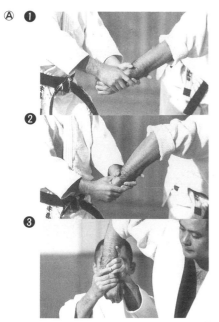

Ⓐ ❶

❷

❸

A. When using the lock to push upward
❶–❸ Having come to the yonkajō position, use uke's wrist as a fulcrum and with the principles of leverage, make the front of his forearm stand up vertically. Because of the power

you have focused into the point on the forearm, apply pressure to the pulse point there. With this control, uke's elbow will go forward.

COMMON MISTAKE
If you twist the wrist, or pull it to the side, the principles of leverage will have no effect. It is important to maintain the leverage position even after you have applied the control.

Ⓑ ❶

❷

B. When using the lock to bring uke down
❶–❷ Holding the hand in yonkajō position, as you move forward, using uke's wrist as a fulcrum turn your left hand over as though covering uke's wrist, and as you apply pressure to the pulse point, push uke's elbow forward.

Focusing the power

Using the little finger as a fulcrum, push forward with the underknuckle of the first finger

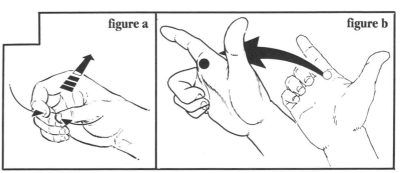

figure a

figure b

If you bring the forefinger and thumb together as in figure **a**, the knuckle of the first finger will be moving away and you will not be able to focus your power.

If you use the little finger as a fulcrum as in figure **b**, and turn the wrist over as though pushing the underknuckle forward, you will focus your power. By using this control together with the movement of the whole body, you will be able to develop large power.

COMMON MISTAKE
It is often the case that in making too much effort to focus the power, sh'te's palm comes away from uke's wrist. If this happens, the principles of the lever can no longer be applied. Right to the end make sure that the palm of the hand is covering the wrist as the focused power is applied.

SHŌMEN-UCHI YONKAJŌ OSAE NI FRONT STRIKE; FOURTH CONTROL II

Use a 450-degree Turn to Bring Your Partner Down

①–② From hidari gyaku-hanmi kamae, use your right arm to block uke's shōmen-uchi.

③–④ Pivoting on your front (left) foot, make a 180-degree turn to the rear, at the same time redirecting uke's power.

⑤–⑧ Slide your left hand down to hold uke's wrist in yonkajō position. As you make a small turn to the rear, thrust uke's arm up, making the elbow go forward.

Uke's Position
As you give in to the pressure that is being applied against your pulse point, your elbow is pushed up and your body "floats."

⑦–⑨ As you make one more large turn in the same direction, turn uke's wrist over to the right side and cut down.

Uke's Position
As sh'te turns your wrist down, your elbow will come forward and you will become unbalanced. Combined with the turning movement, this will bring you to the ground.

⑩—⑪ As your right foot comes forward and your left knee drops to the mat, bring uke to a completely prone position. Apply yonkajō again by pushing forward in front of your stomach. ⑫ Come around so that you are facing across uke's shoulders, change your hand position, and apply the same lock as in nikajō, pinning uke's shoulder.

IMPORTANT POINTS
● Pivoting on the left foot, you make three turns (approximately 450 degrees) while maintaining the same stance.
● In ⑦—⑨, don't have the feeling of just pulling the wrist. Apply the control so that the elbow is pushed forward.

● In the yonkajō lock in ⑪), make sure that you use your hips to bring your balance forward.
● When you are changing the hand into nikajō position, as you change the direction of your body bring your right hand next to your left hand (the side closer to uke's elbow) and grisp uke's forearm, making sure that the angle of his elbow and shoulder doesn't change, pin the back of uke's hand into your left elbow, and bring the right tegatana into uke's elbow.
● When you apply yonkajō, make sure that the palm of your hand doesn't "float away" from uke's wrist.

SUWARI WAZA RYŌTE-MOCHI YONKAJŌ OSAE ICHI / KNEELING TECHNIQUE: TWO HAND GRASP; FOURTH CONTROL I

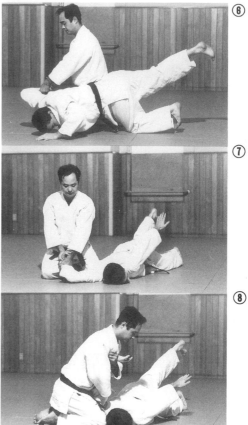

Raise your hands and grasp uke's wrist

①-② Uke grasps both the hands and pulls. Blending with the power of the pull move forward and to the left, bringing your left hand around, palm down, in a circular movement. At the same time, turn the right hand so that the fingers are facing inward, and come in along the line of power of uke's pull, so that the hands that are holding you lose their power.

③ As you move slightly forward to the right with the right knee, bring your left hand around so that it comes outside uke's wrist, then raise your hand in a circular movement so that it holds the wrist in yonkajō position.

④ Move forward slightly one more time along the same line with the right knee, and push uke's elbow forward and up.

⑤ Move along the same line in a big step with the right knee, and as you turn the wrist over cut down, bringing uke to the ground.

⑥-⑦ As you make a step forward with the left knee and then the right knee in the direction of uke's armpit, bring uke to a prone position, and apply yonkajō one more time.

⑧ Change the direction of your body, pin the shoulder, and apply the lock.

UE KARA NO YONKAJŌ OSAE
FOURTH CONTROL LOCK FROM ABOVE
(PRACTICAL APPLICATION)

①

②

③

④

⑤

Drop uke's elbows down using the principles of leverage

① Grasp both uke's wrists from above.

②–③ Using uke's wrists as a fulcrum, apply the power at the point where the underknuckles of your forefingers are touching uke's wrists; thus you can use the principles of leverage to drop uke's elbows down, so that he is brought down and forward.

④ Change the position of your hands so that the direction of the lock is gradually brought around and directed to the opposite shoulder of the hand that is being held. As the yonkajō is applied, uke's elbows will be extended and his whole body will "float" up.

⑤ Note the position of the wrists as seen from the front.

IMPORTANT POINTS

● This is not a matter of pushing uke's wrists downward. Fix your little fingers and use them as a fulcrum, focus the power solely into the underknuckle of the first finger, turn the fingers so that they are pointing downward and cut uke's wrists down. Uke's hands actually remain in the same position; it is the elbows that are brought down.

● Make sure that the palm of your hand does not become separated from uke's wrist.

● If you push your hips forward in such a way that the knot on your belt is pointing downward, your power will be focused in the underknuckle of your first finger.

● The yonkajō that is applied after you have turned the wrists over (④) is in principle the same control as is applied from above (②–③).

SHŌMEN IRIMI-NAGE
FRONT ENTERING THROW

Entry throws are techniques whereby we redirect uke's power and take up a position to his side, and from there attack his hip joint so that he is brought backward and thrown down. If you attack uke's hips from in front of your own body, the technique is shōmen irimi-nage (Front Entry), and if you attack from the side of your own body it is sokumen irimi-nage (Side Entry). Irimi-nage depends on your timing at the very moment that uke comes forward, and for this reason one of its forms is called kokyū-nage (Breath Throw).

If you stumble forward, your instinctive human reaction is to try and raise your upper body, to save yourself from falling over. This is also one of the principles behind shōmen irimi-nage.

Attack your partner from the side

Entry throws are based on the principle of attacking uke's hips from the side. If we were to throw him directly to the rear, he would still have the freedom to move his feet behind him, and so the technique would not be particularly effective. If, however, we throw him diagonally to the rear, although he could take one step away, after that it would then be simple to make him bend at the hips. Thus, if we attack the opponent from the side, he will not be able to resist.

Movement of the arm at the moment of throwing

❶ As you approach from the side, slide your tegatana along the base of the throat, causing uke to bend backward. Make sure that your hand stays in front of your own body. By sliding the hand up as you make the forward movement with your body, you will develop much more power than if you were to use just your arm. On the other hand, if as you move forward you are late with the sliding movement of the arm, none of your power will be transferred into the arm and uke's power will be stronger than yours.

❷ As you move on the diagonal line behind your partner, cut down with your raised hand directly in front of you to throw him. Make sure that you don't come to a position where you are pushing uke's chin or throat.

Using your elbow as a fulcrum, turn the front part of your arm so that the thumb is pointed downward, and at the same time extend the whole arm forward. By applying this control at the same time as you move forward, you will develop strong power.

SHŌMEN-UCHI SHŌMEN IRIMI-NAGE ICHI
FRONT STRIKE: FRONT ENTERING THROW I

In one movement bring your arm to a V position

①–② Come to migi ai-hanmi kamae and make a front strike to uke. Uke raises the right arm and blocks.

③–⑤ As you bring your left foot forward to the left side, open up the body and at the same time turn your tegatana to the outside, redirecting uke's power. As you enter to the side slide your right arm up along the base of uke's throat. With the left hand, catch hold of uke's collar at the same time as he comes forward. All of the above is done as one movement.

Uke's Position
As you are brought forward with the power that blocked the original front strike, sh'te's arm sliding up along your throat causes you to bend backward.

⑥–⑦ As you advance forward with the right foot along the diagonal line to uke's rear, turn your right elbow over so that the thumb of the right hand is pointing downward, extend the whole arm downward, and throw.

IMPORTANT POINTS
● Within the movements ③–⑤, bring your hips to a V position, turning to the right and after that advancing along the front line. This is performed in one movement.

● The arm should be raised in front of the body. If the timing is wrong and the arm is behind you, you will not be able to apply power and you will lose to uke's power (see Common Mistake below).

● For the final throw, the power comes from lowering the center of your own body; the turning over of the elbow is then added to this.

COMMON MISTAKE
One common mistake is that as you move forward with the body, the arm is late so that you end up hanging your arm over uke as you try to throw. Make sure that the arm is in front of your own body as you apply the control.

SHŌMEN-UCHI SHŌMEN IRIMI-NAGE NI FRONT STRIKE; FRONT ENTERING THROW II

As you transfer your weight, slide your arm up

①–③ From hidari gyaku-hanmi kamae, as uke makes a front strike raise your right arm and block.

④–⑥ As you turn your tegatana to the right and redirect uke's power, pivot on the front (left) foot to make a 180-degree turn to the rear. As uke comes forward, hold on to the back of his collar with your left hand.

⑦–⑧ Having completed the turn transfer your weight, making a circular movement with your own body at its center, and lead uke around so that he falls forward and becomes off-balanced.

⑨ With your right fist deliver an atemi to uke's face from below, causing him to raise his upper body up.

⑩–⑪ Transfer your weight from your right foot to your left foot in the same way as in hiriki no yōsei ni, and slide your right hand up along the base of uke's throat, causing him to bend backward.

⑫–⑬ Slide forward with the right foot in a straight line along the diagonal to uke's rear, turn the right hand down, and throw.

IMPORTANT POINTS

● As you make the turning movement uke should be brought around in front of you. You should not be in the position where uke is behind you and you therefore have the feeling of using strength to pull or push uke from the neck.

● Make sure the arm that is raised stays in front of your body as you are transferring your weight from one foot to the other (⑨—⑩). Do not simply use your arm, but rather use the power developed by transferring your weight in order to bend uke over backward. Also, as you bend uke over make sure that you are not leaning on uke to support you.

SHŌMEN-TSUKI SHŌMEN IRIMI-NAGE
FRONT PUNCH; FRONT ENTERING THROW
(PRACTICAL APPLICATION)

Enter in at the moment that uke is bent over

③–④ From hidari gyaku-hanmi kamae, uke comes in and makes a front punch with the right fist. As this happens pivot on the left foot and make a large turning movement to the rear. Bring your right hand up to uke's wrist and blend with the power of the punch. With the left hand grasp the back of uke's collar and lead uke around to the front of your chest.

⑤–⑧ Keeping the weight over the left foot as though you have the intention of moving forward, as uke comes into your chest slide your right hand up along the base of his throat.

⑦–⑩ Slide forward with the right foot in a straight line along the diagonal to uke's rear, turn the right hand over so that the thumb is turned downward, and throw.

IMPORTANT POINTS

● In the basic throw, only after we have caused uke to fall completely forward do we transfer the weight and raise the arm. In the practical application we bring uke around and into the bend of our hips, and we can then slide the arm up without transferring the weight from one foot to the other.

● By dropping our weight over the front foot (thereby making our posture lower), we can add power into the hand that is sliding up.

YOKOMEN-UCHI SHŌMEN-IRIMI-NAGE SIDE STRIKE TO THE HEAD; FRONT ENTERING THROW (PRACTICAL APPLICATION)

Bring uke's arm around into his own neck

①—④ From migi ai-hanmi kamae, as uke attacks with yokomen-uchi turn inside the strike, and as you make a spiralling turning movement use your right tegatana to blend with the power of the strike.

⑤—⑦ Open up your body by moving your right leg to the side, and bring your right hand around with the palm facing downward in a wide movement to the right, so that all of uke's power is redirected to the right side. You should have the feeling that the back of uke's hand is being carried along on top of the back of your own hand. Once you have changed uke's direction, use the left hand to hold on to the back of his collar.

⑧—⑪ Pivoting on the right foot make a large turn to the rear. Keeping the right hands together bring them up in a spiralling movement, folding uke's right hand over so that it comes across his own neck. In this position continue with your turning movement, turn your right hand over so that the thumb is pointing downward, and make the throw.

Uke's Position

As the force of your yokomen-uchi is brought around in a spiralling movement, because of the flow of that line of power your body brings itself around naturally to the final position.

IMPORTANT POINTS

● Perform the technique in one turning movement without stopping the flow of energy.

● All of the turning movement should be done with the right foot at the center.

● Make the spiralling movement while blending with the flow of energy in such a way that uke's hand comes into his neck in a natural continuation of the movement.

USHIRO RYŌTE-MOCHI SHŌMEN IRIMI-NAGE TWO-HAND GRASP FROM BEHIND; FRONT ENTERING THROW (PRACTICAL APPLICATION)

Turn with uke in the same direction

①—③ From migi ai-hanmi kamae, uke makes a front strike, and as you block, uke cuts that hand down and runs behind in an attempt to grab both hands from the rear.

④—⑦ Pivoting on the right foot, make a large turning movement in the same direction as uke. As you turn, bring your right arm up in front of you with a circular movement, turning uke's right shoulder over.

⑧—⑩ Transfer your weight so that your left foot is now at the center and make a large turn to the rear with the right foot. As you cut down with the right hand in a spiral movement, hold on to the back of uke's collar with your left hand and lead him around so that he is in a bent position, and slide your right hand up through the base of his throat.

132

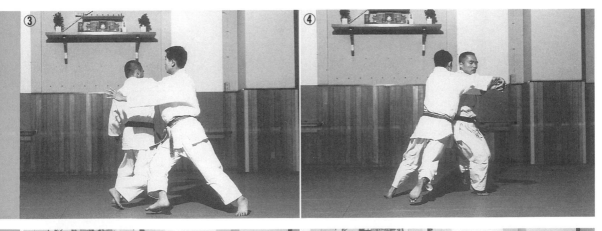

⑪—⑭ Extend forward with the right foot along the diagonal line to the rear of uke, turn the right hand over so that the thumb is pointed downward and throw.

IMPORTANT POINTS
● Make sure that you blend with uke's feeling as he comes behind you to grasp your hand. As you make the turn to face in the same direction as uke, allow everything to happen together with this flow.

RYŌTE-MOCHI SHŌMEN IRIMI-NAGE ICHI
TWO-HAND GRASP; FRONT ENTERING THROW I

Flowing with his power, enter in under uke's arm

① From migi ai-hanmi kamae, uke grasps both your wrists and pulls.

②–③ Blending with the pulling power, bring your right foot forward so that it is in a T position in front of uke's toes, with your hips facing toward the right, and pull the left leg in, bending the knee (the right knee will also bend). At the same time extend your left hand forward with the palm face-up at chest level, and in a circular movement bring the right hand up to face height on the inside of uke's wrist, as though stroking his palm upward.

④–⑤ As the left foot extends forward to the left side, bring both hands up in a circular movement in front of uke's face. As your left hand is still being held by uke's right hand bring

it down over the back of his shoulder blade and allow the little finger to be hooked over uke's wrist. Slide the right hand (still being held by uke's left hand) up in front of uke's other shoulder. The right foot slides across to the left side as the whole body moves.

⑥–⑦ As your right foot slides along the diagonal line to uke's rear, extend both hands and throw.

⑧ This is the front view of the position before entering for the throw. The right shoulder has entered in underneath uke's right arm, and the body is in a low posture.

IMPORTANT POINTS
● The left hand comes into uke's shoulder blade as in tai no henko ichi.
● Blend with uke in such a way that you do not become separated from his hands.

SOKUMEN IRIMI-NAGE
SIDE ENTERING THROW

In sokumen irimi-nage your body is in a "half-on" position as you enter into your partner, and you come from the side of your own body as you close the distance and throw.

Fix the elbow and cut down with the arm

The direction of the throw, in the same way as in shōmen irimi-nage, is along the diagonal line to the rear of uke. As you are making the throw you should not change the direction of the movement, but rather at the moment that you have unbalanced uke to the rear, turn your body so that it is facing along the line of the throw, and then simply extend along that line and perform the throw. At the same time, cut down with the arm that you have brought in to the base of uke's throat. With this control, by coming into a low posture the power that you have developed can be amplified and then transferred into your partner. Be aware that as you extend forward, if you close the distance between your body and your arm you will not be able to transfer the power of your body as you drop your weight downward.

COMMON MISTAKE

It often happens that the hand is pushed to the side as you attempt to make the throw. Because uke's body is standing up, however much force you apply you will not be able to unbalance him.

KATATE-MOCHI SOKUMEN IRIMI-NAGE ICHI
ONE-HAND GRASP; SIDE ENTERING THROW I

Extend forward with the hip joint, and enter in from the side

① From migi ai-hanmi kamae, uke grasps your left wrist and pulls.

②–③ Blending with the pulling movement, come forward with the right foot so that it meets the toes of uke's right foot in a T position, with the weight strongly forward, and pull up the left leg with the knee bent. At the same time, turn the hips to face to the right side and extend both hands palms up, the left hand in front of your chest, the right hand in front of your stomach. You should now be in a "half-on" position in relation to your partner's body.

Uke's Position

As your pulling power is turned into your inside line, your elbow is pushed into the side of your body, which causes you to be unbalanced to the rear.

④–⑥ As you turn your hips to the left, extend your left leg forward to the rear of uke; at the same time bring your left hand around in front of uke's body and enter with it through the base of uke's throat at chest height. The right tegatana

comes along the side of uke's body; make sure that the front of your body is fixed to the side of uke's body.

Uke's Position

As the power that has been redirected to the left side comes round in a circular movement into your neck, you are brought off balance to the rear and bent backward.

⑦–⑧ As your left foot comes forward along the line diagonally to the rear of uke, cut down with both hands and throw, keeping the hands in a palm-upward position.

IMPORTANT POINTS

● Do not extend to the side the hand that is being pulled, but rather change the direction that the hand is pointing in as the direction of the hips changes.

● In position ⑧, by bringing the weight forward strongly over the front foot, you can ensure that uke will not be able to raise his upper body.

● Make sure when you perform the throw that you do not just use your arms to push uke's body down.

● When you make the side entering movement (④–⑤), the back of the left hand should move in a circle as though following the line of the surface of a ball.

Position of the feet in the first movement

Move forward so that your toes are pointed outward, and your foot comes to uke's front foot in a T shape.

When you make the entry from the side, it is common for the body to move forward as though in a straight line. However, the hand should come round in a circular movement, passing in front of uke's body, and then from the fingers enter along the base of uke's throat.

KATA-MOCHI SOKUMEN IRIMI-NAGE NI
SHOULDER GRASP; SIDE ENTERING THROW II

By controlling with the shoulder, turn uke's elbow inward

① From hidari gyaku-hanmi kamae uke, with his hand in an upright position and starting with the little finger, grasps the shoulder of your dōgi and pushes. Rest your left hand on the outside of uke's elbow, with your wrist facing inward.

②–④ Pivot on the left foot to make a turn to the rear of at least 90 degrees. At the same time turn the left hand over so that the palm is facing upward, and extend the arm out at chest height. Together with this movement use the movement of your shoulder to lock uke's hand, which is holding you from the side of the little finger, and as you turn uke's elbow to the inside use your left hand to "scoop" his elbow and thus bring him off balance. Your right hand turns over with the left hand so that the palm is facing upward and is extended out at stomach height.

⑤–⑧ As the left foot advances to the rear of uke, bring the left hand round in front of uke's body and enter deeply through the base of uke's throat, bending him backward. The right hand should be resting across uke's body.

⑦–⑨ Extend the left foot along the line diagonally to the rear of uke, keeping the palms facing up, cut down with both hands, and throw.

IMPORTANT POINTS

● After the first turn, you should be in a "half-on" position facing uke's side line.

● When you make the side entering movement, the back of the left hand should move in a circle as though following the line of the surface of a ball. Be careful of entering in with too straight a movement.

COMMON MISTAKE

When you turn uke's elbow in to the inside it is easy to pull the arm in toward yourself. However, the point is not to apply force to the elbow in order to lock it, but rather to unbalance uke by using the movement of your shoulder, and then adding to that the control with the arm.

USHIRO RYŌHIJI-MOCHI SOKUMEN IRIMI-NAGE ICHI / BOTH-ELBOW GRASP FROM BEHIND; SIDE ENTERING THROW I

Using the elbows as a fulcrum, turn the front of the arms over in a chevron shape.

① Uke comes from behind and grasps both your elbows, and pulls.

②–④ Blending with the pulling energy, turn 180 degrees to the rear with the right foot. At the same time turn both elbows forward so that the palms of both hands are pointing outward.

⑤–⑥ As your left foot comes to uke's rear, turn the direction of your body and at the same time, keeping the palms of the hands pointing upward, cut down and forward with the left hand in a chevron shape. At the end of the move the left hand should have entered deeply through the base of uke's throat, and the right tegatana should be lying along the side of uke's body.

Uke's Position

The palm of your left hand (that is holding sh'te's elbow) is pushed in toward your own elbow so that you are bent backward and off-balanced to the rear.

⑦ As your left foot extends along the line diagonally to the rear of uke, keeping both palms facing upward cut down with both hands, and throw.

IMPORTANT POINT

● In the movement where you change direction and turn your elbows over (⑤–⑧), you should be making use of the power generated from the shifting of balance.

USHIRO RYŌKATA-MOCHI SOKUMEN IRIMI-NAGE NI / BOTH-SHOULDER GRASP FROM BEHIND; SIDE ENTERING THROW II

From this position change the direction of your body, pulling uke forward

① uke comes from behind and grasps your shoulders, and pushes.

②–③ Blend with the energy of the push and move forward from the right foot, bringing both shoulders forward so that the palms of both hands are turned outward, thus unbalancing uke and raising his elbows.

④ Bring the left foot around to the inside in a circular movement so that it passes your center line and moves further to the right.

⑤ Put your weight strongly over your right foot and turn your hips so that they are facing toward the right side, and bring your left elbow up so that it fits into the base of uke's throat as he comes forward. At the same time, make sure that your weight is strongly over the right foot and bend your left knee so that you have a low posture.

Uke's Position

Because sh'te's shoulders have turned around, your hands, which were holding on to the shoulders, have been turned

"inside-out," and so your body has been turned into a "half-on" position and pulled forward.

⑥–⑦ As your left foot extends to uke's rear, turn the palms of your hands face up and, using the elbow as a fulcrum, turn the left hand over and to the front. The right tegatana comes into the side of uke's body.

⑧–⑨ As your left foot extends along the line diagonally to the rear of uke, cut down with both hands, and throw.

IMPORTANT POINT

After you have changed direction ⑤, make sure that your body is not in any way twisted.

SHŌMEN-UCHI SOKUMEN IRIMI-NAGE FRONT STRIKE; SIDE ENTERING THROW
(PRACTICAL APPLICATION)

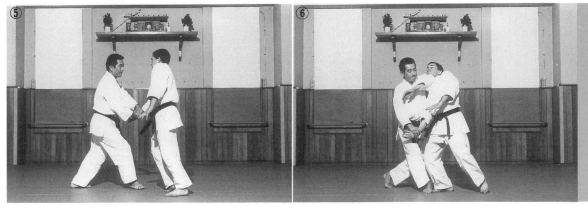

Change the direction of your hips and come together with uke

①–④ From migi ai-hanmi kamae, as your partner strikes with shōmen-uchi bring both tegatana together and move to the inside, redirecting the energy.

⑤–⑧ With your left hand hold uke's right hand at the point where the thumb is attached to the hand and as you bring it across the front of your stomach as though in a cross-cut [with a sword], pull uke forward, and as you do so transfer uke's hand into your right hand. At the same time, bring the right foot forward so that it makes a T-shape with the toes of uke's right foot, and bring your weight strongly over your right foot; as uke is pulled forward bring your left elbow up into the base of his throat.

⑦–⑪ As your left foot extends along the diagonal line to the rear of uke (you are turning into uke's right hip), bring your left hand over and cut down in front of you, and throw.

IMPORTANT POINTS

● In position ⑧, use the turning power of your hips to pull uke forward. Make sure that you are not just pulling uke with your hands.

● In reality, from the moment that you turn uke's hand around, all that follows is done in one movement.

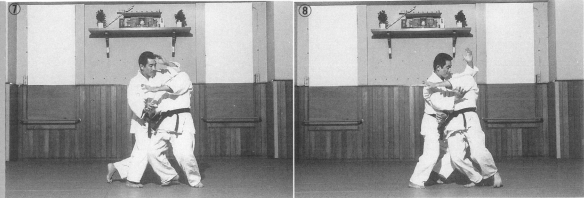

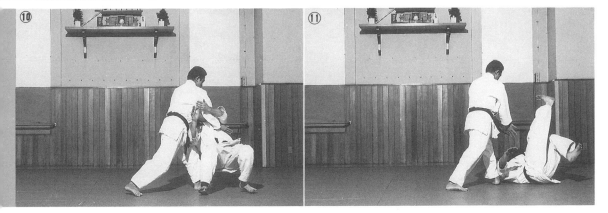

KOTE-GAESHI
RETURN-THE-WRIST THROW

Cut the hand down and over in order to throw

Kote-gaeshi is the technique whereby you turn your partner's wrist over and to the outside so that the elbow is bent inward, and then, by applying the other hand and cutting down deeply you throw him. The purpose is not to lock out uke's wrist; rather, by locking the wrist you will unbalance his body, which will in itself lead to the throw. However, once you have unbalanced uke, if you do not extend his body so that he no longer has the power to stand up, the technique will not be effective.

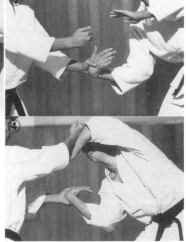

How to turn the wrist over

① Unbalance uke to the front and hold his hand by hooking your little finger over his wrist, and bring your thumb over the back of the knuckle of his little finger—the point where the finger is attached to the hand.

②—③ Make the next movement so that uke's hand stays away from his body. As you pull uke forward, turn his hand over so that it closes over your own little finger. If you turn the hand over in a big movement, uke's body will regain balance as he is pulled forward, so turn the hand over in a small movement in front of your stomach. Also, if you pull the hand too much, uke's arm will straighten out so that it will become

difficult to apply the throw. Therefore, his elbow should be bent just slightly more than 90 degrees.

④ As uke comes forward as the result of having his wrist bent over, deliver a back-fisted atemi to the face with the right hand

CUTTING THE HAND DOWN AND OVER

Slide your hand down in the direction of uke's fingers

After you have turned uke's hand over, bring the palm of your right hand over uke's hand and cut down by sliding your hand down in the direction of uke's fingers. By using this control, uke's elbow will be turned inside and the whole of his body will be unbalanced backward and to the right. If you were to cut down merely by twisting his wrist around to the outside, the lock would not be effective, you would not unbalance the whole of his body, and you would not be able to apply the throw.

Applying the lock

Turn the shoulder over and bring uke to a prone position

① Once you have thrown uke, keep your wrist in the same position, with your fingers pointing inward, and bring the four fingers of your right hand to his elbow.

②–③ As you step around in the direction of uke's head, pull his elbow in so that it is bent in toward you and turn the arm round in a circular movement, keeping the shoulder at the center of the circle. By using this control you can turn his shoulder over and bring him to a prone position. As you are doing this, make sure that you do not relax the control on his wrist that had been cut down.

④ Change the grip of the right hand so that the fingers are now pointing downward, bring your balance strongly over your front foot, and sink your hips straight down, locking out uke's wrist, elbow, and shoulder. As you sink your hips down, at the same time slide your right palm down on the elbow.

SHŌMEN-TSUKI; KOTE-GAESHI NI
FRONT PUNCH; RETURN-THE-WRIST THROW II

Throw through the use of continuous circular movements

①–③ From hidari gyaku-hanmi kamae, as uke comes in with shōmen-tsuki, pivot on the left foot and, blending with the punch, make a turn so that you are in a position 45 degrees to uke's rear, and bring your left hand up to uke's elbow.

④–⑤ As you transfer your balance extend your right hand forward to the front and at the same time slide your left hand down from uke's elbow so that your little finger is hooked over his wrist, and you are holding his hand down by the side of your hip. This is the same movement as the preparatory movement for hiriki no yōsei ni.

Uke's Position

As your body comes forward with the power of the punch the direction of the power is changed, and you are pulled forward and therefore unbalanced.

⑥–⑦ Pivoting on the right leg make a turn to the rear of at least 180 degrees and at the same time turn your left hand over, cutting uke's hand down, and give a right-handed back-fist atemi to the face.

Uke's Position

As your hand is turned over in the kote-gaeshi position, you are pulled forward, and as your body moves forward atemi comes into your face.

⑧–⑩ As you make one more large turn to the rear, use your right hand to cut down deeply on uke's wrist, and apply the throw.

⑪–⑬ As your left foot comes around in a circle and you transfer your weight, use your right hand to move uke's elbow around and bring him to a prone position, control the elbow, and apply the lock.

IMPORTANT POINTS

● The purpose of the movement in position ⑤, is to enable you to blend with uke's power and then bring the whole of the force along in the new direction. The movement is not merely one of pulling the hand. It is designed to bring the whole of your balance forward, and therefore it should also have the effect of pulling uke forward.

● Without consciously trying to hold onto uke's wrist, allow your hand to slide down from his elbow, and your little finger will naturally hook over his wrist.

● To make sure that uke cannot regain his balance, reinforce the feeling of pulling forward, by keeping you balance strongly over you front foot.

● When you are repeating your turning movement from the low position (⑦–⑨), make sure that you fix the front foot correctly so that you maintain a strong posture.

SUWARI WAZA RYŌTE-MOCHI KOTE-GAESHI ICHI KNEELING TECHNIQUE: TWO-HAND GRASP; RETURN-THE WRIST THROW I

① From seiza, uke grasps both your wrists and pulls.

②–③ As you turn your palms up and bring them together, move forward and to the right with the right knee. Bring your left hand across to cover the back of uke's left hand, and as you release your right-hand by turning it to a palm-down position, use your left hand to grip the back of uke's hand in kote-gaeshi. The little finger should be above the wristline, with ring and middle finger gripping the area of the palm below the thumb. The thumb should be just below the knuckle of the little finger.

④–⑧ Bring your right tegatana to the back of uke's left hand, and as you move forward and to the left with the left knee turn your tegatana down to the front, and throw. (The final lock is not shown.)

IMPORTANT POINTS

● **When you turn uke's wrist over, in addition to having the feeling of squeezing your own little finger, use the point where your thumb is attached to your hand to push on the back of uke's hand.**

● **Depending on the flow of power, it would not be considered incorrect if uke's wrist were to be bent in toward the arm, and you were to throw him inward, moving in toward his body, in a way similar to other kote-gaeshi throw techniques.**

Turning over the hand

❶ Bring both hands together, turning them so that the palms are facing upward, and as you bring your left hand underneath your right hand, place your left thumb, at the point where his little finger is joined to the hand, on the back of uke's left hand.

❷ Turn your right tegatana downward so that you slip your hand away from uke's grip, and bring the back of uke's left hand into the palm of your right hand. As the back of uke's hand comes into your palm, use your little finger and the next two fingers of your left hand to naturally grasp uke's hand at the point where his thumb is attached to the hand. Uke should now be in a position where the left elbow is bent inward to the body, and the palm of the left hand is facing outward.

❸–❹ Bring your right tegatana alongside your left thumb, cut down and forward with tegatana, and throw.

Hold the back of the hand from below, turn it over, and throw

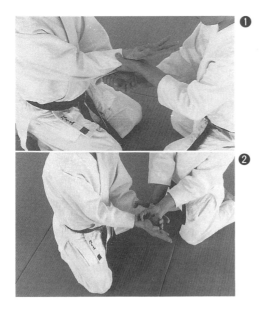

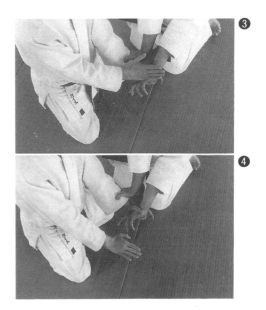

USHIRO RYŌTE-MOCHI KOTE-GAESHI TWO-HAND GRASP FROM BEHIND; RETURN-THE-WRIST THROW (PRACTICAL APPLICATION 1)

Use the movement of the release to turn the wrist over

① Uke grasps both your hands from behind, and pushes.

②—③ As you bring the left foot around in a circle forward and to the right, bring the back of the left hand to the back of your hip.

④—⑧ Bring your balance onto the left foot and make a 180-degree turn to the rear, releasing the left hand that was being held. At the same time, use the right hand in a palm-down position to lead uke's hand, which is holding it, around in a horizontal line, and with your left hand that is now free hold on to the back of uke's right hand.

⑦—⑨ Bring your balance onto the right foot, and as you make a large turning movement to the rear, turn your right hand so that the palm is facing inward, and push forward with your elbow so that your hand is released. If this movement is done correctly, uke's right wrist will now be bent

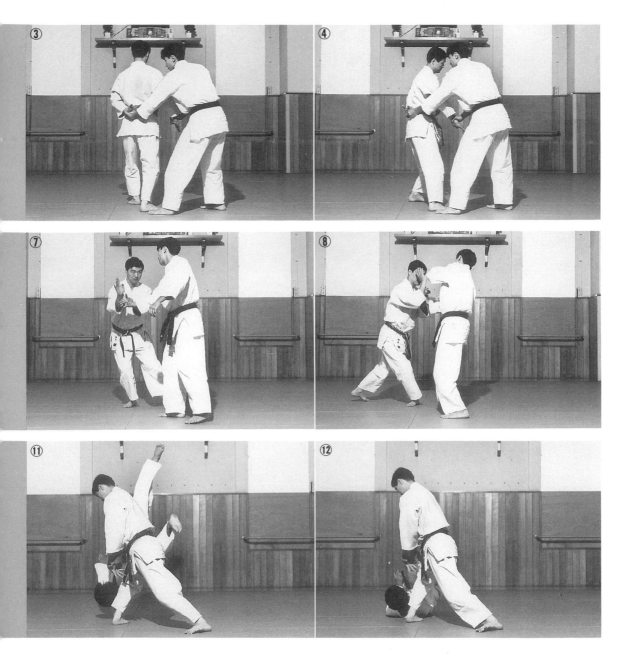

over. The right hand continues in its movement after it has been released, and gives an atemi to uke's face.

⑩–⑫ Pivoting on the right foot, make another large turning movement and cut down deeply with your right hand over uke's wrist, applying the throw.

IMPORTANT POINTS

● By bringing the back of your left hand to the back of your hip, you will loosen uke's grip on the hand. If you then make the turning movement, your hand will be released.

● When you are releasing the second hand, as you turn your palm inward and push forward with your elbow in order to make the release, the inside of your forearm will push up against the back of the hand that was holding it, so that uke's wrist will naturally come to the folded-over position.

USHIRO RYŌTE-MOCHI KOTE-GAESHI TWO-HAND GRASP FROM BEHIND; RETURN-THE-WRIST THROW (PRACTICAL APPLICATION 2)

Come face-to-face with uke by making a small turning movement in the same direction as him

①–③ From migi ai-hanmi kamae, uke strikes with shōmen-uchi, cuts down your hand that has made the block, and runs behind your back in an attempt to grasp both your wrists.

④–⑦ Blending with uke's movement, bring your left foot around in a circular movement and transfer your weight onto your left foot, and as you make the turning movement use your left hand to grasp uke's right hand from the thumb side.

⑧–⑪ Keeping your weight over your right foot, make a large turn to the rear: as you turn your left hand over use your right hand to cut uke's wrist down, and apply the throw.

IMPORTANT POINT

● By turning in the same direction as uke, but moving ahead of him in a smaller circle, you will end up facing him.

● This technique is the same as in Practical Application ①, but in this case the technique is applied before uke manages to grab your wrists.

HIJI-ATE KOKYŪ-NAGE
"HITTING-ELBOW" BREATH THROW

How to turn the elbow over

Turn the elbow over in a circular movement

The method as applied to uke's right elbow is as follows:

❶ Extend your partner's arm so that his palm is facing upward, and grasp his wrist lightly with your right hand. Bring your left arm (also in a palm-up position) so that it comes underneath uke's arm, with the inside of your own elbow touching the back of uke's elbow. In this position make sure that your left hand is in the same shape as in kamae, neither overextended or overbent.

❷ Without changing the basic line from the shoulder to the fingertips turn your left elbow over and extend your arm downward. The fingers of your left hand should now be pointing downward. The right hand should be controlling uke's wrist so that his hand stays in a palm-up position. This control enables you to turn uke's arm forward, while turning his shoulder over, so that he will be unbalanced to the front. Combined with your own advancing movement, uke's unbalanced position will allow you to throw him.

Attack the extended elbow joint

In hiji-ate kokyū-nage, we apply a breath throw sharply against the locked-out elbow joint. Because you can apply this throw in an instant, it is extremely effective as a "counter technique" in a real fight. In addition to the basic technique, in which you bring your own elbow to uke's elbow and then turn it over, there is also the practical application in which, if your opponent punches you, you simply snap his locked-out elbow joint.

IMPORTANT POINTS
● Make sure that you don't just push forward with your elbow, but rather maintain the contact between your own elbow and uke's elbow so that as your elbow moves it will cause uke's elbow to move as well.
● Make sure that you don't allow the distance between uke's elbow and your own body to get too tight.
● Use your right hand to control uke's arm so that he is not able to change its position.

COMMON MISTAKE
If you come from below so that you are just pushing uke's arm straight up, you will not be able to unbalance him.

Practical application of hiji-ate kokyū-nage

Snap the extended elbow

As you enter in and side-step the punch, at the moment that your opponent's elbow is extended you flick ("snap") it with your own elbow. At the exact moment that your elbow meets uke's, turn your own elbow over. This is a dangerous technique, so please be careful when you practice it in training.

KATATE-MOCHI HIJI-ATE KOKYŪ-NAGE ICHI
ONE-HAND GRASP; HITTING-ELBOW BREATH
THROW I

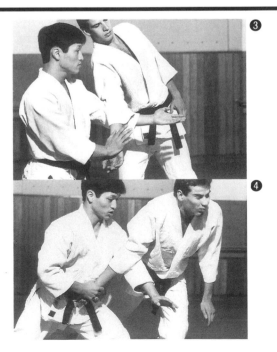

As you release your hand, bring your elbow to meet uke's elbow

① From migi-ai-hanmi kamae, uke grasps your left hand, and pulls.

②–③ Blending with the pulling energy, as you move forward to the right side with the right foot, redirect the energy and release your hand from uke's grasp; at the same time grasp uke's right wrist with your right hand and bring your left hand up in a palm-up position so that the inside of your own elbow comes up against the back of uke's elbow in front of your chest. As you move bring your left foot up so that you are in kamae position.

④–⑦ As you extend forward and to the left with your left foot, turn your left elbow over, and throw.

IMPORTANT POINT

● As you move to the right you release your hand, and as you move across to the left you apply the throw. These movements should be done in the form of an exact V shape.

The Method of releasing the hand

❶ Blend with the pulling power of your partner, and as you move diagonally forward to the right bring your left hand to a palm-up position.

Uke's Position

As your pulling power is redirected to the left, your elbow becomes extended.

❷ As you turn the left hand over to a palm-down position, push forward with your left elbow so that it comes into contact with uke's right elbow. As uke's elbow is in a straightened position and your elbow and uke's elbow become closer together, uke's wrist will be twisted and his hand will release your left hand. From this position, it is important that your left hand passes underneath uke's elbow in order to apply a hiji-ate technique.

❸ As you perform the release with your left hand, bring your right tegatana over the top of uke's wrist, and slide your left arm underneath uke's arm with your hand in a palm-up position so that your elbows meet in an X shape, making sure that the inside of your elbow and the back of uke's elbow are touching each other. All of the above should be done in one movement.

❹ As you move forward diagonally to the left turn the left elbow over, and throw.

157

SHŌMEN-TSUKI HIJI-ATE KOKYŪ-NAGE NI
FRONT PUNCH; HITTING-ELBOW BREATH
THROW II

Throw your partner in the same direction as he punches

①–② From hidari gyaku-hanmi kamae, uke pulls the right foot back and brings the right fist to his side in preparation for the punch. Move forward from the front foot so as to maintain the correct distance (*maai*).

③–④ Blending with the forward movement of uke's punch, pivot on the left foot and make a turning movement to the rear, and at the same time move your own center line away from the line of the punch. As you make this move bring the left tegatana up to uke's wrist in a flowing blocking movement, and use your own turning movement to extend uke's elbow.

⑤–⑥ As you bring your left elbow to uke's right elbow, grasp his wrist with your right hand then bring your left arm underneath his elbow in a palm-up position.

⑦–⑩ As you move forward with the left foot turn your left elbow over, and throw.

IMPORTANT POINTS

● The technique from photo ③ to photo ⑧ should be done in one movement.

● As you avoid the punch you should be roughly parallel to Uke's Position, and you should move along uke's line of energy to apply the throw.

YOKOMEN-UCHI HIJI-ATE KOKYŪ-NAGE
SIDE STRIKE TO THE HEAD; HITTING-ELBOW
BREATH THROW (PRACTICAL APPLICATION)

Open up your body and extend uke's elbow

①–② From migi ai-hanmi kamae, raise your right hand at the same time as uke raises his right tegatana.

③–⑤ As uke cuts down with yokomen-uchi move inside with a flowing block.

⑥–⑦ As you open up to the side with the right foot, slide your left hand down to uke's wrist and redirect his power to the right. As you transfer uke's hand to your right hand, bring your left elbow up to meet uke's right elbow and then slide your left arm underneath uke's elbow.

⑧–⑪ As you move forward and to the left with the left foot, turn your left elbow over, and throw.

IMPORTANT POINTS

● In ⑦, as you open your body to the side, make sure that your balance is over your right foot.

● In ⑥–⑦, your left hand holds uke's hand at the point where the thumb is joined to the hand. As you transfer uke's hand to your right hand make sure that his hand is in a palm-up position, and then extend his elbow.

USHIRO RYŌTE-MOCHI HIJI-ATE KOKYŪ-NAGE
TWO-HAND GRASP FROM BEHIND; HITTING-
ELBOW BREATH THROW (PRACTICAL APPLICATION)

⑤–⑥ Reading uke's intention to grab your wrists, raise both hands into the air from kamae position.

⑦–⑧ Pivoting on the right foot make a turn to the rear, bringing your left hand around in front of your chest. As you then reverse direction by sliding your left leg behind you, use the movement of your left hand (still being held by uke's left hand) to extend uke's elbow in front of you, and bring your right hand underneath uke's left elbow.

⑨–⑪ As you move forward from your right foot, turn your right elbow over and throw.

IMPORTANT POINTS

● Whether uke has actually grabbed your left wrist or only has the intention of grabbing your wrist, by bringing your left hand around in front of your chest you will extend his left elbow.

● By coming round in a circle in the opposite direction to the circle that uke is making, you will feel the possibility of the countermove as you come to meet him.

Make a counterturn and face your partner

①–④ From migi ai-hanmi kamae uke attacks with shōmen-uchi and cuts down on your hand as it comes to block, then runs behind in an attempt to grasp both wrists.

TENCHI-NAGE
HEAVEN AND EARTH THROW

Divide your hands between heaven and earth

In tenchi-nage, from a position in which both hands are being held, you extend the power of your hands both upward and downward to unbalance uke and apply the throw. Rather than depending just on the power of your arms to throw uke, unbalance him so that he is in an unstable position, then throw him by transferring the power of the movement of the lower half of your body through your arms. You can think of this technique as a form of kokyū-nage, and you can in fact create a kokyū-nage out of it.

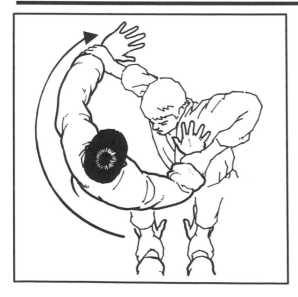

How to redirect the line of power

Lower hand—Keeping the palm of your hand face down, make a circular movement to the front and have the feeling of bring uke's hand around in a circular movement to his rear, keeping his shoulder at the center of the circle. This is not merely a movement with your hand but should be done in conjunction with the circular movement of your lower body.

Upper hand—Slide your hand up on the inside of uke's wrist and toward his armpit, raising his elbow.

Uke's Position
As one of your hands is brought around in a circle you will have the feeling of being turned around the fixed point of your front foot, and will be unbalanced to the rear. At the same time the shoulder and elbow on the other side of your body will be raised up.

RYŌTE-MOCHI TENCHI-NAGE ICHI
TWO-HAND GRASP; HEAVEN AND EARTH THROW I

Fix your partner in an unbalanced position, and then move forward.

① From migi ai-hanmi kamae, uke grasps both your wrists and pulls.

②–④ Move forward and to the left side in a circular movement with your left foot, as though drawing a circle around uke's right foot, and at the same time bring your left hand around in a palm-down position and raise your right hand by sliding it up toward uke's armpit. As the body moves forward your right foot will slide to the rear.

⑤–⑦ As your right foot moves forward diagonally and to the rear of uke, cut down with both hands, so that both thumbs are pointing downward, and throw.

Uke's Position

As you are unbalanced backward and to the rear, you will be holding onto sh'te's left hand for support, and as the hand that you are holding comes around diagonally to your rear, your body will be extended and you will be thrown.

IMPORTANT POINTS

● When your left leg comes around in a circular movement accompanied by your left hand, which also moves around in a circle, it should all be done in one smooth movement. As your body comes to a lower position your hand will also become lower, and it is this that causes uke to be unbalanced.

● When you apply the throw, maintain the posture of your upper body so that both the lower body and the upper body move together. When you transfer your power into uke use both hands equally to extend your power downward.

● When you move forward, make sure that you don't lose the correct distance between your body and your hands.

HIJI-SHIME
ELBOW LOCK

In the hiji-shime technique we fix uke's elbow between our own elbow and our chest, and by turning our hips in a circular movement apply power against the elbow joint in the direction in which it cannot bend, thereby controlling uke. It is not a matter of using your weight to lock the elbow but rather of keeping your arm over your center of balance and applying the force that is created by the turning movement against the elbow.

Keep your arm over your center of balance

① The following explanation applies if the lock is put on uke's right elbow. With your left hand grasp uke's right wrist, turn his elbow forward (as in ikkajō), and fix the elbow against your chest by bringing your left elbow over his elbow. In this position keep your weight over your left foot, so that your arm is over your center of balance.

②–③ Pivot on your left foot, bringing your right foot around to the front right side in a circular movement. As your arm and body also come around in one smooth movement your power will be applied in a horizontal line to the front part of uke's elbow, which had previously been turned over.

④ As you make the turn your stance will become wider and your posture will become lower, so that uke will become unbalanced to the rear and will be forced to crouch down.

IMPORTANT POINTS
● **If you try to push down with your elbow or twist your body, you will not be able to transfer your weight into uke's elbow.**
● **By keeping a strong center of balance as you make the turn, your elbow will develop considerable power.**
● **By making the turning movement and lowering your posture at the same time, you will develop the flowing power of a spiral.**
● **Make sure that your hips are facing directly along your front line right to the end of the technique.**

MUNE-MOCHI; HIJI-SHIME NI CHEST GRASP; ELBOW LOCK II

Cut down the arm and bring it to your chest

① From hidari gyaku-hanmi kamae, uke uses his right hand to grasp both lapels of your dōgi, and pushes. Bringing the lapels together, uke grips both lapels between thumb and forefinger, making sure that the fist is palm-down, and the knuckles are pointing forward.

② Blend with the pushing power and move forward and to the left side with the left foot. As you move and redirect the energy, give a right-handed back-fist atemi to uke's face. The left hand moves in the same way as in katate-mochi techniques, with the palm turned downward.

③–④ With your right hand hold the back of uke's right hand and fix it to your chest. Pivoting on your left foot, make a 45-degree turn to the rear and at the same time slide your left hand up and raise uke's elbow.

⑤–⑧ Pivoting on the left foot, make a large turning movement to the rear; at the same time cut down diagonally with the left hand in a palm-up position so that you cut uke's elbow forward. Once uke's elbow has come underneath your own elbow, hold the wrist with your left hand.

⑦–⑧ Fixing uke's arm to your chest, pivot on the left foot and bring the right foot around in a turning movement to the front, and apply the lock.

IMPORTANT POINTS

● In ④, do not push up on uke's elbow, but fix his hand to your chest ③ and in that position make the turn so that, with the assistance of your left hand, his wrist and elbow are turned over.

● In ⑤–⑧, you should not pull uke's arm so that it comes to your chest but rather have the opposite feeling—push your chest forward so that it comes to meet uke's arm.

KOKYŪ-HŌ ICHI
BREATHING METHOD I

Transfer the movement of your lower body through to your partner

Kokyū-hō is the method whereby, using specific kneeling techniques, we train to develop control of the breath. We learn to use our hands as a pipeline to transfer the movement of our lower body into uke in order to control him. Depending on the way in which uke uses his power, we respond with a particular method of breath control.

① Uke grasps both your wrists from the side, and pulls in a straight line.

②–③ Blending with the pulling power, open up your knees, push forward with your hips, and raise the tegatana of both hands in a circular movement into uke's armpits in the same way as in hiriki no yōsei ichi. As you do this, rise up on your toes.

Uke's Position
As the direction of your pulling power is redirected, your elbows are raised up, and your elbows and shoulders become locked. ④–⑤ Maintain your upper body in the same posture and move to the side from your left knee.

Uke's Position

As sh'te's wrists move to the side, your elbows, shoulders, and hips are locked out, and you naturally become unbalanced.

⑥–⑦ Using your toes to push against the mat, move forward with your knees so that as your upper body also moves forward you unbalance your partner to the rear, and cut down, distributing your power equally between your left and right hands. At the same time, use the energy of your partner as he falls to the rear to pull your lower body in so that it is in a position alongside him. Maintain your posture and keep your power and feeling attached to uke. All of the above should be performed in one action.

Uke's Position

Because you are in a position where your whole body is locked out, as sh'te brings his wrists around you are unbalanced to the rear. And you will be prevented from standing up because sh'te maintains the connection between his power and yourself as he is alongside you.

IMPORTANT POINTS

● The body movement in ②–③ is done by pushing the hips forward. If instead of extending just your arms you come forward with your upper body, you will be in an unbalanced position.

● In ④–⑤, make sure that you don't pull your hands to the side. By locking uke's upper body and then moving to the side, you will be able to move your partner's position without having to move his power. In this way, you will be able to ensure that uke is brought along with your movement.

● It is the same principle in the cutting down in ⑥–⑦. As you push forward strongly with the big toes of both feet, you can use the power of uke falling backward to pull your lower body forward.

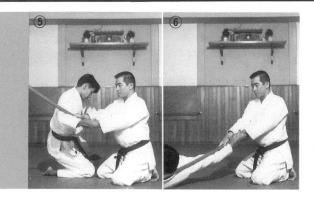

Explanation through use of the sword

Using both hands, use the same movements as though raising up and cutting down with a bokken. Make sure that you do not do this in a straight movement (i.e., lifting straight up and down).

KOKYŪ-HŌ NI
BREATHING METHOD II

Bring uke up and in toward you

① Uke grasps both your wrists and pushes.

②–③ Blend with the power of the push and bring the forearms up in a circular movement toward yourself. Do not raise your elbows but open them slightly. At the same time rise up on your toes.

Uke's Position

As the direction of the power of the push is redirected, you are pulled forward and also raised up.

④ Keeping both hands in the same position, move to the side from the left knee.

⑤–⑥ Straighten your back and cut down using both hands equally. Use the energy of uke as he falls back to pull your lower body in.

IMPORTANT POINTS

● When you have raised both your hands up, the distance between them should be greater than in kokyū-hō ichi.

● Make sure that you do not pull with your elbows.

KOKYŪ-HŌ SAN
BREATHING METHOD III

Drop uke's hips and chest and allow that power to come into your hands

This is a technique that you use when uke has grasped you in such a way that your wrists are completely controlled. You send out your own power and then utilize uke's reaction to unbalance him.

① Uke grasps your wrists from underneath and maintains that position so that whichever way you try to move, he reacts immediately to hold you in the same position.

② With a feeling almost of pulling them in, turn both hands over in a circular movement so that they're in a palm-up position, and then drop them downward. At the same time rise up on your toes.

Uke's Position

By giving the feeling of pulling, sh'te is causing you to react by pulling back in return; by turning your wrists over he is causing you to try to twist your hands back to their original position; by pushing your hands down he is creating the reaction whereby you try to raise them.

③—⑤ With the hands in a palm-up position push them forward in the direction of uke's elbows, turn both your tegatana in a circular movement so that the palms are facing forward, and raise both hands up toward uke's armpits so that you will be in the same position as in kokyū-hō ichi.

Uke's Position

As your hands stay in the same position, your own pulling energy brings them in under your armpits so that the power remaining raises your hands and twists them, causing your upper body to "float" up.

⑥—⑦ Move to the side in the same way as in kokyū-hō ichi, cut down with both hands, and using the power of uke as he falls over, pull your lower body in, coming up against the side of uke's body.

KOKYŪ-HŌ YON
BREATHING METHOD IV

Use the power of your hips to straighten out uke's elbow

① Uke holds both your wrists from underneath in such a way that you are unable to open your elbows.

② Bring both hands to the middle, palms facing upward, with the left hand on top of the right.

Uke's Position

Because you will have the feeling that your hands are being twisted toward the center, as sh'te brings both of his hands to the center your elbows will be turned inward.

③–⑧ Bring your right hand to rest on top of uke's right wrist, and as you turn your hand over so that the back of the hand is facing upward, slide it down toward uke's elbow and then, starting from the little-finger side of the hand, clench your fist. At the same time, make a fist with the left hand and push up toward uke's face. Move forward from the left-knee,

rising up on your toes. All of the above should be done in one movement.

Uke's Position

Because of the movement of sh'te's hands, all of your power is focused into the center of your body, so that you are in a position where the whole of your body is locked. The power of sh'te's hips is then transferred directly into your hips, and as your center of balance moves backward you are thrown to the rear.

IMPORTANT POINT

● In ③–⑧, it is not a matter of merely straightening and extending your arms, but of using the forward movement of the hips to bring the upper body forward; with the power generated by the whole body moving forward, both hands will push out.

KOKYŪ-HŌ GO
BREATHING METHOD V

Bring uke forward by using your own turning movement

① Put both your hands on your knees. Uke grasps both your wrists and fixes them to your knees.

② Keeping the balance over the right knee, make a turn to the rear. As you turn your right hand comes off, the left hand remains fixed to the knee.

Uke's Position

As you are pulled forward through the power that you had been pushing with, the back of your left hand, which is holding sh'te's wrist, is bent backward, so that your grip is loosened.

③–⑥ As the hand that was gripping you becomes loose your right hand is freed. Bring the right tegatana to uke's right elbow, and cut it around in the same direction as the turn, throwing uke down onto his back. All of the above is done as one movement at the same time as you are making the turn.

IMPORTANT POINTS

● Don't make the turn first and afterward make the control with the hands.

● Don't try to apply the control just by moving one of your elbows, but make the turn with your whole body.

● As you make the turn, slightly widen your knees, and make sure that you lead uke forward.

● The hand that uke continues to hold should be left on your knee, and you should not move the hand in order to pull uke around.

SHŌMEN-UCHI KOKYŪ-NAGE 1
FRONT STRIKE; BREATH THROW 1

Kokyū-nage is the name given to the general style of technique in which, without stopping the flow of uke's attacking power, we redirect the line of energy and, applying breath power, make the throw.

Following is an introduction to a number of variations of kokyū-nage.

①–② From migi-ai-hanmi kamae, uke makes a front strike.
③ Move straight forward into uke from the right leg, and open the left foot up slightly to the rear. At the same time cut down the left hand from above over uke's right hand, and strike to uke's neck with the right tegatana.
④–⑧ As you transfer your weight from your right foot to your left foot, bring your right knee to the ground, and apply the throw.

IMPORTANT POINTS
● Because of sh'te's movement and the cutting down of the hand, the power of uke's strike is redirected to his left.
● In this technique we do not attack with the hands and pull in as in a judo-style shoulder throw, but rather use the energy of the hands—cutting forward and down—to apply the throw.

SHŌMEN-UCHI KOKYŪ-NAGE 2
FRONT STRIKE; BREATH THROW 2

① Blending with uke's strike, move in as though inviting the attack.

②–⑥ At the moment that uke commits all of his weight to the cutting down of the hand, slide your body in sideways so that it comes against the base of the foot, and use your hips to sweep the foot away.

IMPORTANT POINT

● If you aim to apply this technique from the beginning, uke will be aware of your intention. Move forward with your body as though to meet the attack, and when uke has committed his body to the strike, then change.

YOKOMEN-UCHI KOKYŪ-NAGE
SIDE STRIKE TO THE HEAD; BREATH THROW

①–② From migi ai-hanmi kamae, as uke comes in with yokomen-uchi, move in with the right foot so that you come to meet the joint of his hip.

③ Blending in with uke's cut down, keep your balance over the right foot and open up your body to the rear. At the same time bring your right hand up so that it comes in under uke's right arm. Bring your left hand up so that it locks uke's arm to your body.

④–⑧ As you transfer your weight from your right foot to your left foot, turn your right hand over in the same way as in hiji-ate kokyū-nage, bring your right knee to the ground, and apply the throw.

IMPORTANT POINTS
● Use the power of uke's cut down as you make your own spiralling movement.
● By turning over your elbow, you ensure that you will be transferring forward-moving energy into uke, rather than pulling him into you.
● Make sure that you do not lose contact (*ma-ai*) between yourself and uke.

SHŌMEN-TSUKI KOKYŪ-NAGE
FRONT PUNCH; BREATH THROW

①–③ From hidari gyaku-hanmi kamae, as uke comes forward with a front punch, make your own entering movement and scoop up uke's right arm from underneath with your right hand.

④ As you open up your body bring uke's arm around in a large circle.

⑤–⑧ As you bring your right foot around behind uke lower your own body, cut down uke's hand in a diagonal line, with the feeling of sweeping his foot away, and throw.

KATATE-MOCHI KOKYŪ-NAGE
ONE-HAND GRASP; BREATH THROW

①—⑤ from migi gyaku-hanmi kamae, at the moment uke comes to grasp your left hand, use the same movement as in tai no henkō ni and make a 180-degree turn, keeping your balance over your left foot, redirecting uke's energy.

⑧—⑦ As you open up to the left side with your left foot, turn your left hand to face palm downward, and bring your right tegatana to rest on the inside of uke's elbow.

⑧—⑫ Move forward in a big step with the right foot, making sure that uke keeps his grip on your wrist, turn your right tegatana forward, and throw.

IMPORTANT POINTS

● Once uke has had his power redirected and is moving forward into you, you will be in a position to apply your own countermove.

● Do not just use your right hand to push and make the throw, but rather bring the whole of your body lower and transfer your weight into uke's arm.

RYŌTE-MOCHI KOKYŪ-NAGE
TWO-HAND GRASP; BREATH THROW

①—④ From hidari gyaku-hanmi kamae, as uke comes in to grasp both hands, at the moment that he grasps turn both hands over so that the left hand is palm up and the right hand is palm down; keep your weight over your left foot and make a 180-degree turn as in tai no henko ni, and redirect the energy.

⑤—⑧ As you open up by moving to the left side with your left foot, bring your left hand around in front of you palm down, and bring the right hand up to head height, so that it is on the outside of the hand that is grasping it.

⑦—⑩ Move forward in a big step with the right foot, making sure that uke maintains his grip on both of your wrists, cut down in a circular movement with the right hand while extending forward with both the left and the right hand, and apply the throw.

IMPORTANT POINTS
● When you cut down with the right hand, make sure that the elbow continues to point forward.
● When you throw, if you allow your hand to get behind you, you will not be able to move uke. Make sure that as you move forward and throw, both hands are maintained in position in front of your body.

KATA-MOCHI TEKUBI-KIME KOKYŪ-NAGE
SHOULDER GRASP; WRIST-LOCK BREATH THROW

Lock out the wrist by using your shoulder

①–② From hidari gyaku-hanmi kamae, blending with uke's energy as he comes forward to grasp your shoulder with his hand in a vertical position, move to the left side, redirecting uke's energy, and at the same time give an atemi to his face with your right hand.

③–④ With your right hand fix uke's hand to your shoulder, keep your weight over your left foot and make a turning movement to the rear, and bring your left arm from underneath in a scooping movement with the palm facing upward.

Uke's Position

Your wrist will be turned over so that the back of your hand and the little finger will be trapped against sh'te's shoulder.

⑤–⑥ As you move forward from your left foot, turn your left arm over so that the thumb is pointing downward in the same way as in hiji-ate kokyū-nage, locking uke's wrist and applying the throw.

Uke's Position

Sh'te's shoulder, which had scooped up your wrist from underneath in ④, makes another movement ⑤ so that the wrist comes to a vertical position, and with your wrist in that "turned out" position your elbow is extended, and so your wrist is locked out.

USHIRO RYŌTE-MOCHI JŪJI-NAGE
TWO-HAND GRASP FROM BEHIND; CROSS THROW

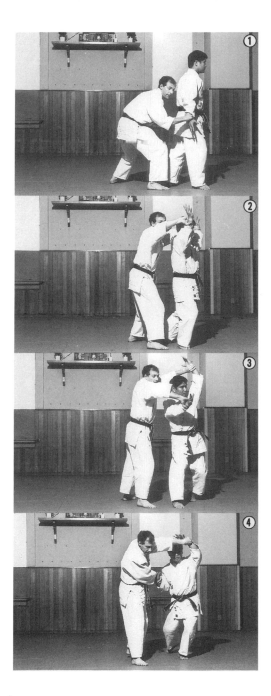

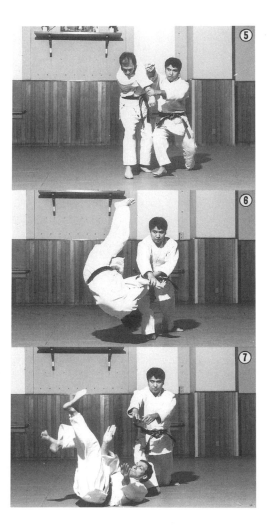

Cross both of uke's elbows over into a cross position

①–② As uke comes from behind and grasps both of your wrists and pulls, pivot on the right foot to the right and raise both hands as though moving around the outside of an egg.

③–④ As you drop both hands down to the front, keep your weight over your left foot and pull your right foot back. Bring your right hand underneath uke's right wrist in a circular movement so that you scoop uke's wrist up between your thumb and forefinger, and lock elbow against the back of uke's left elbow in a cross position. With your left hand grasp uke's left wrist.

⑤–⑦ As you move forward from the right foot, use your right hand to extend uke's right wrist forward, lock out the elbows in the cross position, turn the left shoulder forward, and apply the throw.

KATATE-MOCHI KAITEN-NAGE
ONE-HAND GRASP; CIRCULAR THROW

①—④ From hidari gyaku-hanmi kamae, as uke comes forward to grasp your left hand, make a 180-degree turn as in tai no henkō ni, and redirect the energy.

⑤—⑧ Move around in a circular movement with the left foot to the left side, turn the left hand over and down to the left side, so that it is in a palm-down position.

⑦—⑧ Continuing the movement bring the left hand up in a circular movement so that it is at head height, and keeping your weight over your left foot, begin to make a large turn to the rear.

⑨—⑩ Making a circular movement, the arm that uke is gripping is brought down past your hip, and as it reaches your hip the right hand is brought to uke's neck.

⑪—⑬ Release your left hand so that uke's wrist is scooped up between your thumb and little finger, and as you extend

your left arm forward toward uke's back, throw him with the circular power.

IMPORTANT POINT
● If when you throw you bring uke's right arm toward his shoulder, he will not be sufficiently unbalanced, so make sure that you bring the arm over his back.

SHŌMEN-TSUKI USHIRO-NAGE
FRONT PUNCH; THROW FROM BEHIND

Entering in, grasp the shoulders from behind

①—④ As uke comes in with a front punch, enter in and turn round behind him, and grasp his shoulders.
⑤—⑧ Using the fact that uke's lower body is moving forward, pull back on the shoulders and bring him down.

IMPORTANT POINT
● When you move in, make sure that your own body is not too far away from uke's.

GOSHIN WAZA
SELF-DEFENSE TECHNIQUES

"If you say that person's technique is fast . . . that person is slow,"
you are only seeing the form of the people. You must scrap such thoughts.
In blending with the person's energy (timing),
at the moment when you are really together with that person,
both fast and slow are gone.
This is what Ueshiba Sensei called "becoming one with nature."

— **Gozo Shioda Sayings (IV)** —

USHIRO KATATE-MOCHI KUBI-SHIME SANKAJŌ RENGYŌ-HŌ

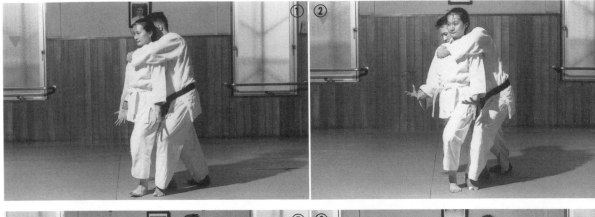

Bend the wrist and press down on the elbow

By inflicting sudden pain you make uke powerless, and you then have the possibility of applying the arrest technique.

① Uke comes from behind, grasps your right wrist with his right hand, and uses his left hand to lock the neck.

②–③ In the same way as in ushiro techniques involving a pull, as you change the direction of your body turn your hands up so as to redirect the energy, bring both hands up in an circular egg-shaped movement, and cause uke to "float."

④–⑤ As you turn your right foot to the inside, keep your balance over that leg and slide your left leg to the rear, at the same time cutting down and forward with both hands. With your left hand grasp uke's right hand, which had been holding on to your own right hand, in sankajō position.

⑥–⑦ Transfer your balance from the right foot to the left, using the power of your body as it changes direction to apply sankajō.

ONE-HAND GRASP FROM BEHIND WITH NECK LOCK; THIRD CONTROL ARREST TECHNIQUE

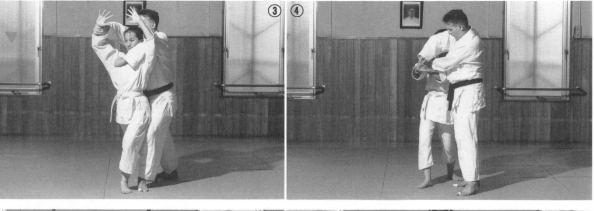

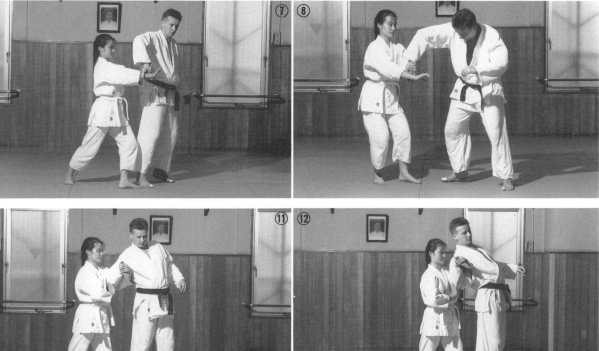

⑧–⑨ As you slide back your left foot, cut down with your left hand in the direction of uke's back, and at the same time bend his wrist. Your right hand grasps uke's elbow.

⑩–⑫ As you move forward from the left leg, use uke's elbow as the axle and cut up and forward with the bent wrist. Use the power of your forward motion to apply sharp pain. (In the picture above there is the added movement of the turn). By taking away uke's power to resist, you are now able to make the arrest.

IMPORTANT POINTS

● Do not pull uke's bent wrist in toward yourself; rather, apply the power of moving forward into the elbow. You should also have the feeling of pushing the elbow down into the wrist.

189

TANTŌ-DORI SHŌMEN-TSUKI HIKI-KIME— SOKUMEN IRIMI-NAGE

Fix the elbow and extend the lower arm forward

①—④ In migi ai-hanmi kamae, uke holds the tantō with the end pointing up, slides the right foot back, then thrusts forward. Turns to the inside and, keeping the balance over the right foot, open up the body. Slide the lower part of your right arm underneath uke's arm, and, as your left foot makes a large turn to the rear, redirect the energy of the strike.

⑤ As you open up with your right foot to the right side, lead uke's right hand around in a circular movement in front of your hips, extending the whole of his body. Slide your right hand down and grasp uke's wrist.

⑥—⑧ As you move forward from the left foot, bring uke's arm forward so that the elbow is stretched out and the hand is in a palm-up position. At the same time bring your left arm over the top in a circular movement so that it then goes underneath uke's elbow, and with your left hand grasp uke's right wrist.

TAKING AWAY THE KNIFE: FRONT THRUST; ELBOW LOCK / SIDE ENTERING THROW

⑨ Using your left forearm, which is underneath uke's elbow, as a fulcrum, extend both your arms forward, locking uke's elbow. ⑩–⑫ As uke's body starts to "float," bring your left foot behind uke, release your left hand and apply sokumen irimi-nage. As you do so take the knife with your right hand.

IMPORTANT POINTS
● As you bring uke's arm around in ⑤, turn the point of the knife away from yourself by twisting uke's wrist around, thereby making sure that you are not in danger of being cut.

● In ⑤, in order to ensure that you are not stabbed by the tantō as you lead uke's arm around, twist uke's wrist so that the tantō is pointing away from you.
● When you apply the elbow lock, close your armpits and make sure that your left arm (which is the fulcrum for the lock) doesn't move, and use both hands to extend uke's lower arm forward.

SHŌMEN-TSUKI KUBI-SHIME
FRONT PUNCH; NECK LOCK

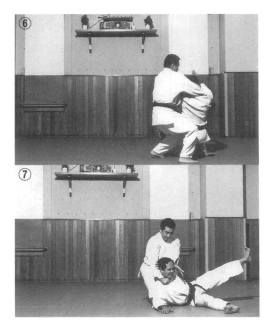

Redirect the punch and come behind uke

①–③ As uke comes in to punch with the right fist, from migi hanmi enter inside the punch by making a large turning movement, and use your right hand to redirect the punch around to the right side, thereby making uke turn the other way.

④–⑤ From behind uke, slide your right hand up across the front of his neck and hold onto the left inside collar of his dōgi; slide your left hand up underneath his left armpit and bring it to the back of his neck.

⑥–⑦ Keeping your balance over your left foot make a turn to the rear, bringing your left knee to the ground and pulling uke back and down. The right hand pulls in around the throat.

IMPORTANT POINTS
● **Pull your right hand in and come to the locking position by using the power of the turning movement.**

KATA-MOCHI SHŌMEN-TSUKI KOKYŪ-NAGE
SHOULDER GRASP WITH FRONT PUNCH; BREATH THROW

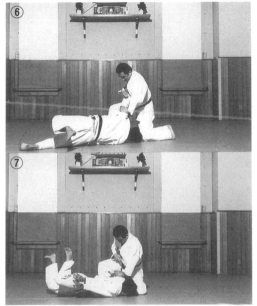

Avoid the punch and throw uke forward

① From hidari ai-hanmi kamae, uke grasps your shoulder with his left hand and makes a punch to your face with his right fist.

②—⑤ As you turn your upper body away to avoid the punch, transfer your balance from your left foot to your right foot and drop your body down, bring your left arm underneath uke's left arm, turn your elbow over and apply the throw.

⑥—⑦ Grab uke's left arm in your left hand, and as you turn it around in a circular movement to the right pulling uke to a prone position, lock the shoulder.

IMPORTANT POINTS
● Don't try to deal directly with uke's punch, but rather, as you avoid the punch, use the power of uke's forward motion in order to apply kokyū-nage.

● When you avoid the punch, be careful that you are not just using your upper body to "run away."

TANTŌ-DORI SHŌMEN-UCHI IKKAJŌ OSAE
TAKING AWAY THE KNIFE: FRONT STRIKE;
FIRST CONTROL

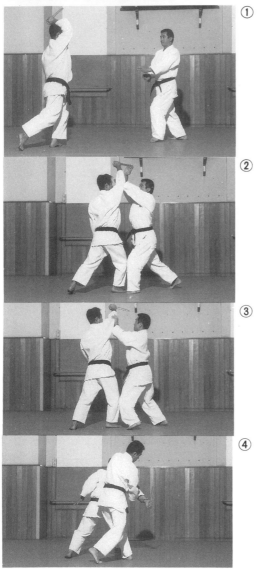

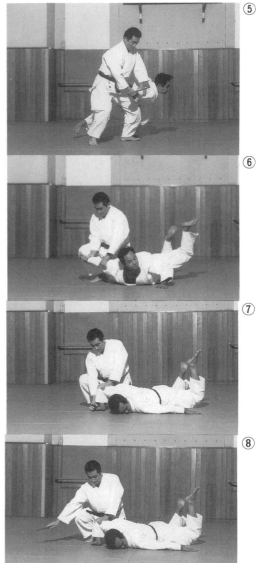

By changing your grip with the right hand, avoid the knife

This technique is used when uke holds the knife in an "opposite grip" (i.e., with the knife held point-down), and strikes down as in a shōmen-uchi.

①–② As uke comes in to make the strike, move straight forward in hidari gyaku-hanmi kamae and block with both hands in a cross position, so that the thumbs of both hands are facing in opposite directions.

③–⑧ Using the same redirection as for yokomen-uchi, turn uke's arm over to the right, and as in ikkajō ni, keep your balance over your left foot and make a 180-degree turn to the rear, then transfer your balance from your left foot to your right foot and bring uke to a completely prone position. In order that your wrist is not cut with the knife, as you pivot to the rear from ③ turn uke's right hand over so that the palm is facing up, and then grasp uke's wrist.

⑦–⑧ Bend uke's wrist into his own armpit, and take the knife.

IMPORTANT POINTS
● When you change your right-hand grip (②–③), do so by sliding the palm of your hand around.
● The position of the last move, when you bend uke's wrist over, is the same position as in the sankajō arrest technique.

TANTŌ-DORI SHŌMEN-TSUKI SHIHŌ-NAGE KUZUSHI / TAKING AWAY THE KNIFE: FRONT THRUST; FOUR-DIRECTION THROW

Avoiding the knife, cut down in a diagonal movement

①–② As uke comes in to thrust with the knife, make a large turning movement to the rear so that you come inside the line of the strike, and re-direct the attack.

③ As uke becomes overextended, grasp his wrist, and as you open up to the side with your right foot lead uke around to your right.

④–⑧ Maintaining your hold on uke's wrist, raise both hands up and bring your left foot forward, changing the direction of

your body. As you bring your left knee to the ground, cut down with both hands in a diagonal line, and apply the throw.

⑦–⑧ Control uke by pinning the elbow, and take the knife.

IMPORTANT POINTS

● When you move your left foot in ④, do it in such a way that your balance stays over your right foot.

● When you make the throw, if you throw in a straight line there is the danger that the knife could stab you in the stomach, so you apply it in a diagonal line in order to keep the knife away from you.

TANTŌ-DORI SHŌMEN-TSUKI UDEGARAMI-NAGE TAKING AWAY THE KNIFE: FRONT THRUST; ARM-LOCK THROW

Cut straight down with uke's arm

①–③ As uke makes a thrust with the tantō, step to the outside of his arm and redirect the attack. As his body becomes overextended grasp his wrist with your right hand and bring your left hand to his elbow.

④ Keep your balance over your right leg and open up by bringing your left foot in a large step to the rear. Pull in uke's elbow with your left tegatana and bend his arm.

⑤–⑦ Transfer your weight from your right foot to your left foot, cut down with both hands in front of you, and apply the throw.

⑧ Pull uke around to your left and turn him over on his shoulder, bringing him to a prone position, and take the knife.

IMPORTANT POINTS

● When you make the throw, bring your right elbow so that it is fixed to the inside of uke's elbow, and then cut down as though you are pushing forward with your elbow.

● Make sure that the throw is done along your own front line, and don't do it in such a way that your right shoulder is out of position.

KEN-DORI SHŌMEN-UCHI HIJI-ATE KOKYŪ-NAGE
TAKING AWAY THE SWORD: FRONT STRIKE; HITTING-ELBOW BREATH THROW

Extend uke and take the hilt of the sword

①–③ From hidari gyaku-hanmi kamae, blending with the front strike that uke makes with the sword, enter in along your front left line and as you avoid the sword open up your body to the rear.

④–⑤ At the moment that you make uke's body flow forward, slide your left hand down between uke's hands to hold the sword and grasp the hilt with your right. At this point,

your left elbow should be fixed to uke's right elbow.

⑥–⑧ As you move forward from your left leg, turn your left elbow over, control uke's right elbow against the joint and as you apply the throw, take the sword.

IMPORTANT POINTS
● Make sure that you do not pull in toward yourself with the hand that is holding the hilt of the sword.
● As you turn your left elbow over, make sure that it continues to be fixed to uke's elbow.

197

KEN-DORI SHŌMEN-UCHI KOSHI-NAGE TAKING AWAY THE SWORD: FRONT STRIKE; HIP THROW

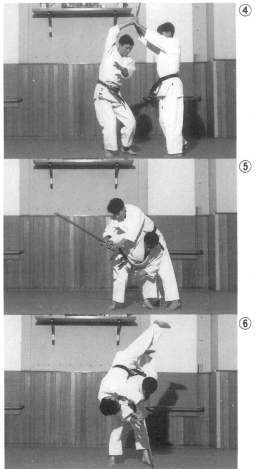

Transfer your center of balance and throw your partner over

①–② As uke comes in and makes a front strike with the sword, avoid and move inside the strike, and take the hilt of the sword with your right hand.

③ Keep your balance over your right foot and open up by moving your left foot in a large step to the rear. As you do so shift your body (hip toward uke) while leading him toward you. (Move your hips in and under uke's in preparation for the throw.)

④–⑤ Maintain your grip on the hilt of the sword and raise your right hand, move forward in a large step with the left

foot so that you enter right into uke, and bring uke over so that he is riding across your hips.

⑥ Using the power generated by transferring your balance from your left foot to your right foot, throw uke into the air, and as you apply the throw, take the sword.

IMPORTANT POINTS
● If you try to simply pull the sword in toward yourself (②) the flow of energy will be interrupted, so lead uke around in such a way that his hand that is holding the sword does not lose its grip.

● When you make the throw, use the spring of the lower body rather than depending on the hand that is pulling.

ŌGI
HIDDEN TECHNIQUES

It is said that aikido is the Way of Harmony.
I think it is simple to explain this saying.
If you face someone, and you can make that person's animosity disappear,
by your own true character,
This is the Harmony of Becoming One. This is not a compromise.
Harmony is a matter of having strength yourself, and then making the other your ally.
He becomes your partner. This is "making harmony in opposition."
But, unless you accumulate virtue, it is impossible.
To sum up, the foundation is your own inner strength.

— **Gozo Shioda Sayings (V)** —

HEADMASTER GOZO SHIODA'S DEMONSTRATION

Once uke has committed his power, you can unbalance his body

Aikido is the Way of Harmony

Aikido is a martial art that has its roots in, and has developed from, a koryū-jujutsu (classic jujutsu) that was practiced by Shinrasaburo Minamoto no Yoshimitsu in the fourteenth century in Kyoto. His techniques were passed on to the Takeda family and became daito ryu jujutsu, and in the Edo period they were brought to Aizu in northern Japan. In Aizu a "palace" martial art called oshikiuchi was also being taught. During the Meiji period Sokaku Takeda

combined the arts of daito ryu and oshikiuchi, and thus was born daito ryu aiki-jujutsu.

Morihei Ueshiba, founder of aikido, became Sokaku Takeda's outstanding student. Ueshiba was also a student of many other martial arts, and was a strong believer in the ideas of the Omoto religion. From the *budō* that he created within himself, founded what we now know as aikido. He taught that aikido is not simply a fighting art

By completely controlling uke's power, you can throw him even while he is still grasping you

Understand the essence of techniques

(*budō*), but a way of purification that has the purpose of bringing together the body and spirit (*kokoro*) in accordance with universal principles. It may be described as the *budō* that has as its purpose the realization of harmony.

I entered the Ueshiba Dōjō in the seventh year of the Showa period (1932) and have trained in aikido for over fifty years; it is only recently that I have come to understand the lessons that Ueshiba Sensei taught us.

In aikido, depending on the power of the other person, there are many basic techniques available to us. Even though the order of each technique is different, the principle that flows through all of the techniques is the same, for example, the stability of the body, changing the balance, leading the energy, and so on.

By controlling the center of uke's palm, where he had focused the power of his grip, you can "bounce" his body

People who come to train in Aikido are often interested in the individual techniques—how can I apply second control, how can I make kote-gaeshi more effective, etc.—but the true purpose of the training is to understand the techniques' common principles.

Once you have completely grasped these principles, you will naturally lose interest in the specific details of individual techniques. Then, depending on the individual circumstance, you will naturally adjust to each situation, and therefore you will have the ability to respond in whichever way is best for you. This means that instead of thinking "I will do this, I will do that," you will come to a level where, because you have a grasp of the principles, you own body will move by itself according to those principles.

By controlling uke's power with your hips, you can control his elbows and unbalance him

By becoming yielding, you will "read" the other person

The most important thing in aikido is what is called "yielding." Usually a human being thinks "I will do this, I will do that," and he is not be able to become "yielding." In that case, whatever he does will result in collision with the person opposite him.

If you can look at the other person with an open heart, without ego, you will be able to see the other person's situation: What he is aiming for, what power he is using, where his balance is, what his feeling is and so on—all will become clear. This cannot be understood by looking

By using the difference in power on the left and right side, you can lead each person in the appropriate direction

with your eyes or trying to understand through intellect. You must understand in an instant, with your heart. If you can realize the other person's situation and can guide it, then it is a simple matter to lead it to your own benefit. If you wish to be yielding when you are facing your opponent, you must be in a perfect stance. If you can do that, you will feel free and easy.

By transferring the power that is used to lift you up down into uke's knees, you can unbalance them

Harmonizing with your opponent

These "secrets" of aikido can be applied to the behavior of people. By correcting your own position, and by making contact with the other person with a spirit of yielding, you will be able to grasp his spirit. At that moment, harmony is born.

In Aikido we don't have competitions, and that is the reason why we don't have a contest of winning or losing.

The purpose of aikido is to realize harmony, through rooting the principles of techniques inside ourselves, without the thought of conflict. As twelfth century *budō* master Kiichi-hogen said, "Harmonize with that which is opposing you," and it might be said that aikido is the Way of realizing this saying.

Gozo Shioda—Sayings

IYAF DOJO LISTING

International Yoshinkan Aikido Federation

2-28-8 Kamiochiai, Shinjuku-ku, Tokyo 161-0034 Japan   Phone: 81-3-3368-5556   Fax: 81-3-3368-5578

Aikido Shudokan

INSTRUCTOR: Joe Thambu
4 Gooch Street, Thombury, Victoria   Australia
Phone: 61-39-480-1570   Fax: 61-39-460-3102

Aikido Yoshinkan Brisbane Dojo

INSTRUCTOR: Michiharu Mori, Shuko Mori
10 Ferry Road, West End, Brisbane   Australia
Phone / Fax: 61-73-255-0155

Aikido Yoshinkan NSW

INSTRUCTOR: Darren Friend, Peggy Woo
Sydney   Australia
Website: www.aikido-yoshinkan-NSW.com

Kanryukan Dojo

INSTRUCTOR: Amos Arad Badash
Melbourne   Australia

Shinbukan

INSTRUCTOR: Tony Arnold
PO Box 1211, AyrQueensland 4807   Australia
Phone: 61-77-831-523

Shinobukan Dojo

INSTRUCTOR: David Dangerfield
The Aikido Institute Inc. PO Box 185
Nambour, Queensland 4560   Australia
Phone: 61-75-445-9116

Yoshinkan Aikido Watanabe Dojo

INSTRUCTOR: Darren Hee Skelton
Badminton Association od, WA Kingsway sporting complex, Kings Road Maddeley   Australia
Phone: 61-89-250-0322

Hikari Dojo

INSTRUCTOR: Eduardo Pinto
Rua 66 no. 56, Pargue Continental, Osasco Sao Paulo, 06020-110   Brazil
Phone: 55-11-3768-06-36 or 55-11-3682-13-75

Konyokan Dojo

INSTRUCTOR: Osamu Ikeda
Rua Padre Leonidas, Da Silva no. 39, Jundiapeda Mogi Das Cruzes SP   Brazil
Phone: 55-11-4727-28-28

Aikido Yoshinkai Bulgaria

INSTRUCTOR: Nencho Smilov
Vozkresenie Blvd., bl.35, en.B, ap. 103 Sofia   Bulgaria
Phone: 359-2-23-24-34

Aiki Budo Centre

INSTRUCTOR: Jaimie Sheppard Ashley Hennessey
650 Elizabeth (east of Adelaide St.), London, Ontario N5Y 3P4   Canada
Phone: 1-519-646-8482 or 1-519-646-3454
Main Street London, Ontario N6P 1R1   Canada
Phone: 1-519-652-9888

Aikido Yoshinkai Burnaby

INSTRUCTOR: Robert Mustard
7671 Edmonds Street, Burnaby, BC V5E 3N1 Canada
Phone: 1-604-786-2334   Fax: 1-604-527-8918

Aikido Yoshinkai Canada

INSTRUCTOR: Takeshi Kimeda
399 Yonge Street, 2nd Floor Toronto, Ontario M5B 1S9   Canada
Phone: 1-416-585-9602

Buseikan Dojo

INSTRUCTOR: James Murray
Buseikan Dojo c/o James Murray 63
Nicole Marie Ave Barrie Ontario, L4M 6Y7   Canada
Phone: 1-705-739-7342

Bushido Club

INSTRUCTOR: Dave Stinson
5030 Maingate Dve, Mississauga, Ontario   Canada
Phone: 1-905-453-6459   Fax: 1-905-873-6133

Bushinkan Dojo

INSTRUCTORS: Jim Arsenault
Martial Arts Room, Recreation Centre (Sth Side)
Canadian Forces Base Trenton, Ontario   Canada
Phone: 1-613-475-4730 or 1-613-392-2811

Buyoukan Dojo

INSTRUCTOR: Louis Bournival, Nadine Auger
Viscount Alexander Park, Community Centre,
Ottawa, Ontario   Canada
Phone: 1-613-742-1264   E-mail: augfam@inexpress.net

Buyukan Dojo

INSTRUCTOR: Michael Chambers
Durham Region Aikido
27-570 Westney Rd., South Ajax, Durham,
Ontario L1S 6V6   Canada
Phone: 1-905-767-2180

Chudokan Dojo

INSTRUCTOR: Kevin Blok
1089 Tecumseh Road East, Windsor, Ontario N8W 1B3
Canada
Phone: 1-519-253-6667   Fax: 1-519-978-3583

Hiryukan Dojo

INSTRUCTOR: Stephen Ohlman
347 Bayfield Street, Unit #4
Barrie, Ontario, L4M 3C3   Canada
Phone: 1-705-722-3004

Jinbukan Dojo

INSTRUCTOR: Roger Plomish
McMaster University and Ottawa Street
YWCA Hamilton, Ontario L&H 3Y9   Canada
Phone: 1-905-544-3129

Kodokan Dojo

INSTRUCTOR: Duncan James
Barrie Aikido Yoshinkan 15 Cedar Pointe
Dr. Unit #20 & 21 Barrie, Ontario   Canada
E-mail: duncanjames1@rogers.com

Kokoro Aikido Dojo

INSTRUCTOR: Eric Sheffield, Debra Mcallister
3600 Kingston Road, Scarborough, Ontario   Canada
Phone: 1-416-234-2766 or 1-416-234-5289

Koshinkan Dojo

INSTRUCTOR: Danny M.D. Ervin
1332 Beattie Street North Bay, Ontario PIB 3T4
Canada
Phone: 1-705-840-1233

Makotokan Dojo

INSTRUCTOR: Steve Nickerson
941 Old French Rd., Kingston, Nova Scotia B0P 1R0
Canada
Phone: 1-902-765-3272
E-mail: aikido@ns.sympatico.ca

Renbukan

INSTRUCTOR: Jim Jeannette, Sue Jeannette
3226 Walker Rd., Windsor, Ontario N8W 3R8
Canada
Phone: 1-519-966-2297   Fax: 1-519-966-8953
Email: aikicen@mnsi.net

Renseikan Dojo

INSTRUCTOR: Ward Jardine
1885 Clements Rd #211
Pickering, Ontario L1V 1N9   Canada
Phone: 1-905-427-8883   Fax: 1-905-831-4793
E-mail: Dojo@Renseikan.com

Reishinkan Dojo

INSTRUCTOR: Alistair James Sumner, Jennifer Le Foreistier
2345 Yonge Street, Ground Floor
Toronto, Ontario M4P 2F5   Canada

Seibukan

INSTRUCTOR: Gary Casey
3565 Queen St., Windsor, Ontario N9C 1N8   Canada
Phone: 1-519-256-7373

Seibukan Dojo

INSTRUCTOR: Tim Webb, Rod Rhem, Brad Middleton
Sealy Park Scout Hall, 115 Main St., South,
Waterdown, Ontario L0R 2HD   Canada
Phone: 1-905-521-3682
E-mail: TheWAY@canada.com

Seibukan Dojo

INSTRUCTOR: Takey Leung
3063 Peter St. Windsor, Ontario N9C 1H2
Canada

Seidokan Dojo

INSTRUCTORS: Fred Haynes, Jim Stewart
Georgetown Memorial Arena, 358 Delrex Blvd.,
Georgetown, Ontario L7G 4H4   Canada
Phone: 1-905-873-6676   Fax: 1-905-873-6133

Seikokan Dojo

INSTRUCTOR: Mark Lemmon
3901 Huron Church Road Windsor,
Ontario N9E 2E4   Canada
Phone: 1-519-966-7263

Seimeikan Dojo

INSTRUCTOR: Mitsugoro Karasawa
2115 Midland Ave., Unit #7
Scarborough, Ontario M1B 3V4   Canada
Phone: 1-416-609-2681   Fax: 1-416-298-3316

Seiwakan

INSTRUCTOR: Greg West, Chris Snowden, Alan Burnett
3106 Autumn Hill Crescent, Burlington,
Ontario L7M 1Y6   Canada
Phone: 1-905-335-6988   Fax: 1-905-332-4356

Sendokan Dojo

INSTRUCTOR: Nic Mills, John Havey, Dawn Rusch
Etobicoke Olympium 590 Rathburn Road
Toronto, Ontario M9C 3T3   Canada
200m past the 2nd light west of HWY 427

Seikeikan

INSTRUCTOR: Fred Springer
2360 Ravine Gate Oakville, Ontario L6M 4R1
Canada
Phone: 1-905-469-4979

Shinbukan

INSTRUCTOR: Wendy Seward
Apt 4, 98 John St., West, Waterloo, Ontario N2L 1C1
Canada
Phone: 1-519-741-5632

Shinseikan Dojo

INSTRUCTOR: Alister Thompson
1290 Queen Street West Toronto, Ontario M6K 1L4
Canada

Shinwakan

INSTRUCTOR: Chuck Bates
580 Grosvener Ave., London, Ontario N5Y 3T3 Canada
Phone: 1-519-642-7321

Shobukan Dojo

INSTRUCTOR: Paul M. Thobo-Carlson
JJ Par Recreation Centre Cold Lake, Air Force Base,
4 Wing, Cold Lake, Alberta T9M 2C6   Canada
Phone: 1-780-8400-8000 #4480

Shouwakan Dojo

INSTRUCTOR: Karen Orgee
Royal Military College 547 Quail Court,
Kingston, Ontario K7M 8Z4   Canada
Phone: 1-613-384-6634

Sowakan Dojo

INSTRUCTOR: Keith Taylor
1410 Toronto Pl., Port Coquitlam, B.C. V3B 2T7
Canada
Phone / Fax: 1-604-944-9329

Tenwakan Dojo

INSTRUCTOR: John Owens
Strathroy, Ontario   Canada
Phone: 1-519-246-9797

Goryukan

INSTRUCTOR: Malcolm Crawford
96 Bosmere Gardens, Emsworth, Hampshire PO10 7NR
England
Phone: 44-124-343-1212

Joseikan Dojo

INSTRUCTOR: Gadi Shorr
Rickmansworth Hertfordshire,
Little Chalfont buckinghmshire   England
Phone: 01923-720534 or 07816-988685,
07977-169561

Kenshinkai

INSTRUCTOR: Garry Masters
5 Hollybank Close, Horndean
Waterlooville, Hampshire PO8 9ES   England
Phone: 44-239-242-6519

Meidokan Dojo

INSTRUCTOR: David Rubens
Unit 11A, The Arches, Maygrove Road
London NW6 2EE   England
Phone: 44-207-372-9866   Fax: 44-207-372-9877

Seishinkan

INSTRUCTOR: Paul Stephens
Intercharge Studio Dalby St. London
Kentish Town Police Station Holmes Rd. Kentish Tow
NW5 8SL   England
Phone: 44-171-267-9421   Fax: 44-171-482-5292
E-mail: paul.eva@virgin.net

Sendokan

INSTRUCTOR: Terry Harrison
Edgware Senior School, Green Lane, Edgware Middlesex
England
Phone: 44-181-953-7971

Shinwakai Dojo

INSTRUCTOR: Jack Poole, Marill Poole
6 Holtspur Way, Beaconsfield, Bucks HP9 1DX
England
Phone / Fax: 44-494-671-666

Taidokan Dojo

INSTRUCTOR: Antony Yates
39 Cherry Tree Rise, Walkern, Hertfordshire   England
Phone: 44-170-760-7100   Contact Dave Rendall

Ukinkan Dojo

INSTRUCTOR: Peter Janko
9 Duke Street WatfordHerts WD1 2PB   England

Aikido Yoshinkai de France

INSTRUCTOR: Jacques Muguraza
Centre D'animation Rene Binet Paris 18 Nord
66, rue René Binet 75018, Paris   France
Phone / Fax: 33-1-39-46-52-29

Aikido Yoshinkan eV

INSTRUCTOR: Hiromichi Nagano
Auenstr. 19, D-80469 Munich   Germany
Phone: 49-89-2012297

Junseikan Dojo

INSTRUCTOR: Stephan Otto
Sportschule FFB-Puch GmbH Am Fuchsboben 9
82256 Fuerstenfeldbruck   Germany
Phone: 49-81-4123026

Shudokan Indonesia

INSTRUCTOR: Mark Hadiarja
JL Terusan Padasaluyu Utarai /12
Bandung 40154 West Java   Indonesia
Phone: 62-22-2002-666   Fax: 62-22-2002-888

Aikido Yoshinkan Shudokan Dojo

INSTRUCTOR: Ramlan Ahmed
6-2, Jin Dagang SB 4/2 Tmn Sg. Besi Indah 43300 Seri
Kembangan, Selangor Darul Ehsan   Indonesia

Aikido Yoshinkan Israel

INSTRUCTOR: Alon Cohen
1: Tel-aviv Dizingof center
2: Petach Tikva (kats 3t)
Phone: 052-3-286128

Aikido Yoshinkan of Israel

INSTRUCTOR: Gadi Shorr
Samurai Dojo 5 Corazin St. Givatayim   Israel
Phone: 972-3-9585817   Fax: 972-3-5707265

Daitokan

INSTRUCTOR: Certa Tonino
via Solario 14, 20100 Milano   Italy

Yoshinkan Firenze

INSTRUCTOR: Christina Beretta
c/o Beretta-Casella via G.di Vittorio, 42
I-50029 Impruneta Firenze   Italy
Phone: 39-55-2020086

Aikido Yoshinkan Malaysia

INSTRUCTOR: Sonny Loke
11-A, Jalan Jejaka Dua, Taman Maluri,
Cheras Kuala Lumpur 55100   Malaysia
Phone: 9-60-3-9200-1080   E-mail:
yoshin@tm.net.my

Mushinkan Dojo

INSTRUCTOR: Francis Ramasamy
No. 30 Kim Blan Aik Road, Penang 10400   Malaysia
Phone: 9-60-4-226-9309

Mushinkan Dojo

INSTRUCTOR: Rama Krishnan K.G.
Training center, Tingkat 2, Bangunan MPJBT,
Jalan Dedap 14, Taman Johor Jaya,
81100 Johor Bahru, Johor   Malaysia

Shoreikan Dojo

INSTRUCTOR: Tony Chung
32-3, Jalan Prima 2, Rusat Niaga, Metro Prima,
Kepong, 52100, Kuala Lumpur   Malaysia
Phone: 9-60-1-9336-5320

Seishinkan Dojo

INSTRUCTOR: Raymond Cutajar
HIBERNIANS Sports PAVILLION Corradino Heights,
Poala   Malta
Phone: 356-21-38-87-34

Ryusuikan

INSTRUCTOR: Christian Sommer
Body Plan Sport Krachtenveld 28 3893 te Zeewolde
Netherlands
Phone: 31-36-522 2418   Fax: 31-36-522-253

New Zealand Yoshinkan Aikido Centre

INSTRUCTORS: Eddie Wong
Mt. Albert Recreation Centre, 773 New North Rd.,
Mt. Albert, Auckland   New Zealand
Phone: 64-9-828-5422

Bugenkan Dojo

INSTRUCTOR: Tomasy Orylski
Zespol Szkol Technicznych UL,
Kosciuszki 5 Rybnik   Poland
Phone: 48-50-144-5168

Bumeikan Dojo

INSTRUCTOR: Rafal Rzepus
Gimnazjum Nr 4 (Secondary School No. 4)
UL. Graniczna 46, 40-863 Katowice   Poland
Phone: 48-60-503-3244   Fax: 48-32-352-3112

Busenkan Dojo

INSTRUCTOR: Bogdan Sukowski
Gimnazjum nr. 13 UL. Zamehofa 15
41-200 Sonoweic   Poland
Phone: 48-32-291-8702

Koyokan

INSTRUCTOR: Aleksander Nawrat
ZSB UL. Bojkowska 16, 44-100 Gliwice   Poland
E-mail: olek@yoshinkan.pl

Koyokan Dojo

INSTRUCTOR: Aleksander Nawrat
Silesian University of Technology
UL. Konarskiego 22, 44-100 Gliwice   Poland
Phone: 48-32-50491-1969   Fax: 48-32-276-1929

Hagakurekan Dojo

INSTRUCTOR: Oleg Kupriyanov
Russia, Moscow Truzjenikov, Pereulok, 16/17
Russian Federation
Phone: 741-2255

Misogi kan

INSTRUCTOR: David G. Eayres
Academy of Eastern Martial Arts
Culture House 8, Letnikov Street Moscow
Russian Federation
Phone: 7-095-237-50-83   E-mail: sensei@co.ru

Mujestvo Dojo

INSTRUCTOR: Gutorov Leonid
Russia S-Petersburg, Raevskbgo Str, 16
Universitetskaja 7/9   Russian Federation
Phone: 7-812-557-4265

Russia Seibukan Rashid Dojo

INSTRUCTOR: Rashit Gataulin

Seibukan

INSTRUCTOR: Rustam Karimov
Dojo 1, Ochakovskaya Street, House 9
Dojo 2, Shamsheva Street, House 8
Saint Petersburg   Russian Federation
Phone: 7-812-108-33-57

Seifuhkan Dojo

INSTRUCTOR: Zdachaev Vasilii
413840 Rossia Saratov REG, Balakovo Str
Mendeleeva dom 11   Russian Federation
Phone: 7-845-3-3567-19

Shorei Dojo

INSTRUCTOR: Grigoriev Nikolay
Rossia S-Petersburg, str Raevskogo 16
Universitetskaja 7/9   Russian Federation
Phone: 7-812-5525-993

Typhoon Dojo

INSTRUCTOR: Podoinikov Andrey
Rossia, Novosibirsk city, Polevaya-5 str,
Russian Federation
Phone: 7-8913-914-7835

Aikido Yosshinkan Siam Shindokan

INSTRUCTOR: Geordan Reynolds
Pattaya Beach   Thailand
Phone: 66-9062-1107
E-mail: Reynolds@yoshinkan.com

Academy Aiki Bujutsu

INSTRUCTOR: Alexandre Kozulovsky
Ukraine, Lvov Chukarina Str 3,
School N25 Aikido Yoshinkan Dojo   Ukraine
Phone: 38-032-221-5817

Kiev Ukuraine Dojo Kiyokan

INSTRUCTOR: Andriy Berensinny
Kiev   Ukraine
Phone: 38-067-775-83-48
E-mail: kiev_yoshinkan@ukr.net
Website: www.yoshinkan.kiev.ua

Agatsukan Dojo

INSTRUCTOR: Richard Lopez
2543 New York Ave., Whiting, IN 46394   USA
Phone: 1-219-659-2370

Budokan

INSTRUCTOR: Dennis Jiminez
28 Molle Street West Babylon, New York 11704   USA
Phone: 1-631-587-2636 or 0291
Fax: 1-631-587-0291

Doshinkan Dojo

INSTRUCTOR: Utada Yukio
5836-38 Henry Avenue Philadelphia, PA 19128   USA
Phone: 1-215-483-3000

East County Budokai

INSTRUCTOR: Cameron T. Garry
2782-E Sweetwater Springs Blvd.,
Spring Valley, CA 91977   USA
Phone: 1-619-300-3187, 1-619-421-2170

Eishinkan

INSTRUCTOR: Randy Stoner
29821 Aventura, Suite C
Rancho Santa Margarita, CA 92688   USA
Phone: 1-949-713-3343   E-mail: info@eishinkan.com

Fudokan Dojo

INSTRUCTOR: Robert Parker
8303 W. 126th Street, Suite D Overland Park,
Kansas 66213   USA
Phone / Fax: 1-913-681-2120

Higirikan Dojo

INSTRUCTOR: Masatoshi Morita
1405 Huntington Avenue, Unit 8 South
San Francisco, CA 94080   USA
Phone: 1-650-345-1501 or 1-650-872-2968

Kadokan Dojo

INSTRUCTORS: Sam Combes
1510 South Euclid Ave., Anaheim, CA 92802   USA
Phone: 1-714-774-5730

Meishinkan Dojo

INSTRUCTOR: Kevin Bradley
Meishinkan Dojo c/o Rife's Martial Arts 92,
Barney Drive Joliet, IL. 60435   USA
E-mail: aikidorat@hotmail.com
        kevin.bradley@mcd.com

Renseikan Dojo

INSTRUCTOR: Alvin McClure
Keewaydin Center 3030 E. 53rd Street,
Minneapolis, MN 5541   USA
Phone: 1-612-889-2098   Fax: 1-612-297-7261

Sanbukan

INSTRUCTOR: Mitsu Yamashita
3311 W. Artesia Blvd. Long Beach, California   USA
Phone: 1-562-531-2301
E-mail: info@sanbukan.com

Seigokan Dojo

INSTRUCTOR: Richard Essick
PO Box 5414 Chicago, IL 60680   USA
Phone: 1-630-236-0000   E-mail: msp4@prodigy.net

Seikeikan Dojo

INSTRUCTOR: Steven Miranda
6745 Hazel Ave. Orangevale, CA 95662   USA
Phone: 1-916-989-6023

Seishinkan Dojo

INSTRUCTORS: John Parks Tom
1681 Auburn Rd., Rochester Hills, MI 48307   USA
Phone: 1-248-853-7555

Shidokan

INSTRUCTORS: Dewitt Cooper
2447 Townsquare Dr., Jacksonvile, FL 32216   USA
Phone: 1-904-724-5740

Shindokan Dojo

INSTRUCTOR: Geordan Reynolds
17661 Beach Blvd., Huntington Beach, CA 92647   USA
Phone: 1-949-495-9216

Shinkokan Dojo

INSTRUCTOR: Delfin Labrador
PO Box 231953, Anchorage, AK 99523   USA
Phone: 1-907-336-2988   Fax: 1-907-344-8770
E-mail: budo@ptialaska.net

Shinrikan Dojo

INSTRUCTOR: Leslie Mills, Teddie Linder
6844 Hawthorn Park Dr. Indianapolis, IN 46220   USA
Phone: 1-317-579-9055

Shiseikan Dojo

INSTRUCTOR: Herman Hurst
19480 Livernois Detroit, MI 48221-1760   USA
Phone: 1-313-365-8945

Shobukan

INSTRUCTOR: Greg Berg
1735 Kings Rd., Vista, CA 92084   USA
Phone: 1-760-717-5655

Shoshinkan Dojo

INSTRUCTOR: Jesse Nichols
3610 W. Liberty, Ann Arbor, MI 48106   USA
Phone: 1-734-913-1072
E-mail: jdn@movementlearning.com

Shuharikan Dojo

INSTRUCTOR: Jon Sharratt, Gordon shumaker, Glen
Giacoletto
265 West 7th St., 3rd flr. St. Paul, MN 55102   USA
Phone: 1-651-222 7337

Shuseikan Dojo

INSTRUCTOR: Terrenyce Cooper
4745 Dundee Circle, Jacksonville, FL 32210   USA
Phone: 1-904-779-7767

Shuwakan Dojo

INSTRUCTORS: Christopher Howey, Evely Dysarz
5129 E. 65th St., Indianapolis, IN 46620   USA
Phone / Fax: 1-317-251-2070

Takudokan Dojo

INSTRUCTOR: Stephen Hamilton
PO Box 4909 Sunriver, Oregon 97707   USA
Phone: 1-541-598-8654

Tenmeikan

INSTRUCTOR: Leonard Takahashi
17237 Reimer St., Fountain Valley, CA 92708   USA

University of Kentucky Aikido Club

INSTRUCTOR: Keisuke Mizuno
University of Kentucky Lexington,
Kentucky 40506   USA

Aikido Yoshinkan Takadanobaba Dojo

6F Utagawa Bldg., 2-16-6 Takadanobaba,
Shinjuku-ku, Tokyo 169-0075   Japan
Phone: 81-3-3207-0341   Fax: 81-3-3207-0349
E-mail: yoshinkan-baba@oregano.ocn.ne.jp
URL: www1.ocn.ne.jp/~yoshin03/

Features living facilities for those who wish to train
intensively in order to open branch dojos throughout the world.